SUPERNATURAL
PENNSYLVANIA

Laurie Hull

Schiffer Publishing Ltd®

4880 Lower Valley Road · Atglen,Pennsylvania 19310

Schiffer Books are available at special discounts for bulk purchases for sales promotions or premiums. Special editions, including personalized covers, corporate imprints, and excerpts can be created in large quantities for special needs. For more information contact the publisher:

Published by Schiffer Publishing Ltd.
4880 Lower Valley Road
Atglen, PA 19310
Phone: (610) 593-1777; Fax: (610) 593-2002
E-mail: Info@schifferbooks.com

For the largest selection of fine reference books on this and related subjects, please visit our web site at **www.schifferbooks.com**
We are always looking for people to write books on new and related subjects. If you have an idea for a book please contact us at the above address.

This book may be purchased from the publisher.
Include $5.00 for shipping.
Please try your bookstore first.
You may write for a free catalog.

In Europe, Schiffer books are distributed by
Bushwood Books
6 Marksbury Ave.
Kew Gardens
Surrey TW9 4JF England
Phone: 44 (0) 20 8392-8585; Fax: 44 (0) 20 8392-9876
E-mail: info@bushwoodbooks.co.uk
Website: www.bushwoodbooks.co.uk

All photos unless otherwise noted are by the author
Ouija is a registered trademark of Parker Brothers
Copyright © 2010 Laurie Hull

Library of Congress Control Number: 2010931146

Designed by RoS
Type set in Baveuse /New Baskerville BT

ISBN: 978-0-7643-3606-5
Printed in China

Dedication

Dedicated to the spirits that walk among us;
may they find peace.
Also to the Jane Doe found near the Twin Tunnels;
may you be, someday soon, known by your true name
and may your murderer be caught
and brought to justice.

Acknowledgments

Special thanks to my family for their understanding of and patience with my obsession with all things spooky. My husband, Pauric, has the patience of a saint and has spent so many nights standing in a dark, spooky place with me as I try to make contact with spirits there. Thank you to my parents who never doubted my abilities and perceptions. Thanks to my editor and friend, Dinah Roseberry, for her neverending faith in me. I am eternally grateful to my friends and associates at Tri-County Paranormal, especially Bill Horton, Lori Clark, and Rich Hickman. Finally, sincere thanks are extended to Adele Gamble at New Hope Ghost Tours, Sam Slaymaker at Rock Ford, Rick Fink at Cliveden, and all others who shared their stories and photos.

Contents

Introduction

After all of my travels to traditionally haunted places like London, England, Ireland, Nova Scotia, New England, and California, Pennsylvania is, in my opinion, the most haunted place I have encountered. Nearly every community has its ghostly legends, from Native Americans to modern murder victims. The ghosts of Pennsylvania walk our roads, lurk in our historic museums and restaurants, and live in our homes.

Some have asked me, "Why do you see ghosts all the time? Why do they talk to *you*?" The answer is simple. I look for them and seek them out. I explained it to a bed and breakfast owner this way: Ghosts are people without a physical body. If a person came into an establishment and was very busy and did not invite conversation, the host would likely let them go about their business and not interact with them any more than necessary. However, if a person came in and chatted with the host, seemed interested in the place and its history, and wanted to get to know them, the host would likely talk to them, tell them stories, give them a tour, and interact with them whenever their paths crossed. Ghosts are like us. They are not going to seek out interaction with people who repel it or treat them badly.

The locations featured in this book are truly haunted, though not all are haunted by ghosts. Some are haunted by things other than ghosts. They seem to be full of a strange energy that surrounds the place and affects those who are sensitive to it. Others are haunted by rumor and legend. They are haunted by a memory of a past tragedy or resident. Pennsylvania is so full of these places it would be impossible to include them all in one book. I have assembled a collection of places that people who want to experience that strange energy will find it.

Spooky Streets

ost of the time, streets are the ways we travel to and from work, school, and the hundreds of other places we visit in our daily lives. At other times, these same byways have an entirely different feeling. A lonely car on a dark road may be met by floating lights, ghostly hitchhikers, or scenes from the past.

13 Bends · Alpsville

Tracking down the exact location of "13 Bends" was quite a task. After months of research and interviews, I am still not positive I have actually found it, but what I have concluded will be presented here.

The legend is fascinating and lures carloads of teenagers and others in search of a spooky thrill out to the suburban hills that surround the city of Pittsburgh. I narrowed the possible locations of 13 Bends down to Campbell's Run Road in Harmarville or Coulterville Road in Alpsville.

The Legend

There is a dark, steep, twisty road known as 13 Bends. It is a one-lane road with 12 bends going up and 13 going down. At the top of this hill there was an orphanage. The orphanage caught fire and all of the orphans burned to death. Today, all that remains are the foundations of the building and the ghosts. Visitors to the site have reported everything from floating lights to disembodied screams of children and full-body burning apparitions.

The Orphanage

Of the three sites I had zeroed in on, only one had an orphanage in its history. This was in Alpsville. There was an orphanage next to the St. Patrick Church, which still stands on 3rd Street. The orphanage didn't burn down, though. There was a fire that destroyed the church in 1924[1], but no one was injured in the fire, let alone killed. At the time of the fire, the orphanage was standing, but had been converted to a private home. The old orphanage was demolished in 1950, but St. Patrick's Church is still there. Like many of the places in this part of Pennsylvania, when the mining industry died, the people left. The church no longer operates as a church and is owned by a private non-profit corporation called Bigley Family Cemetery and it may be in danger of being demolished. The cemetery is not in good shape; many of the markers are missing and quite a few are overturned. If you decide to visit this church and grounds in search of the ghosts of 13 Bends, please be respectful and obtain permission.

And it just may be worth your while to get permission to visit, because if reports and photos are to be believed, there *is* something up there. Visitors to the site have reported activity at all hours of the day and night. There are unexplained spikes in electromagnetic field readings, equipment malfunctions, and battery drains; all classic indicators of paranormal activity.

Campbell's Run Road

There was never an orphanage here. This is an old windy road that leads to an abandoned mine. As creepy and tempting as that sounds, there are no disasters or accidents associated with it yet. **It is illegal to trespass there after dark** and if thrill-seekers keep going up, there just might be a good ghost-spawning disaster. Among the pitfalls one may encounter while trespassing are an "acid pond, caustic soda facility, and a shaft to the mine itself".[2]

What about Renzie Road?

Some internet accounts of this legend name the site of 13 Bends as Renzie Road in Elizabeth Township. So far, the only reason I can find for Renzie Road being tagged as 13 bends is that it is steep and windy. No reports of anything paranormal or supernatural have ever come from this area, nor was there ever an orphanage there.

Mist forming at 13 Bends.

Cossart Road - Chadds Ford

Cult House, Devil's Tree, and Satanville

The stories about this place seemed incredible; a huge mansion with windows shaped like inverted crosses, a road where all the trees grew away from it, a tree with roots shaped like skulls... Into this mix was occasionally added murderous dark-colored SUVs that chased explorers down windy "Cult House Road" in "Satanville."

If you have been to this area, you probably know that there is no "Cult House Road" and no "Satanville." The road that is known as Cult House Road is actually Cossart Road. There are no houses on this road with inverted cross windows. The trees *do* grow away from the road, however, but that is because they have been trimmed to keep the limbs away from power lines. I have seen videos of people who claim to have filmed themselves being chased down Cossart Road. This is more likely a carload of teens enjoying scaring the life out of someone than a ghostly or demonic SUV.

At Close Range

Does this out of the way road have a bad reputation just because of bored kids or is there a more sinister source for its seeming spookiness? The partial answer to this may lie in the events portrayed in a movie, *At Close Range*. This movie is a dramatized account of events that occurred in the area in 1978.

That summer was the Johnston Brothers' reign of terror. During their crime spree, they murdered and buried three junior members of their gang right off Cossart Road, in the middle of what was then a huge estate. The three young men buried there were 20-year-old Wayne Sampson, 17-year-old Duane Lincoln, and gang ringleader Bruce Johnston's 18-year-old stepson, Jimmy Johnston. According to the gang member who led police to the gravesite, Jimmy was "still gurgling when he was thrown into the hole after being shot"[3] by his own stepfather.

A fourth junior member, who is still missing, is Jimmy Sampson, Wayne's 24-year-old brother. Although an informant swore to having witnessed Jimmy being shot and then buried at a local landfill, he was unable to locate the grave and the body has never been found. Another area murder attributed to the gang was that of a thief who had been shot by Bruce and buried near the Stottsville Tavern.

Are these murders the source of the spookiness? Does the shadow of that summer of murder still hang over Cossart Road? Two questions remain unanswered from this whole mess.

The first is: "Where is Jimmy Sampson buried?"
The other question is, "What happened to the gang's money?"

The millions they acquired from their crimes are said to still be hidden somewhere in the area.

A trip down Cossart Road during the day shows the place for what it is. Just like most of the other back roads in Chadds Ford, the view from it is mainly of fields with a couple of houses here and there.

It is easy to see how at night, especially to those unfamiliar with it, Cossart Road could be very scary. Even during the day, the road is full of unexpected twists that require careful navigation. To add to the whole experience, the day I went, I had my teenage daughters with me. They heard I was going to "Cult House Road." Apparently, they had heard all about Satanville, freaky trees that grow away from the road, and the general creepy stuff there. They wanted to see the Devil Tree and the Cult House. I warned them that the reality of the place was likely not as exciting as what they'd heard.

I stopped at the dead end that lead to Cossart Road to take photos and heard a chorus of screams from the car. My daughters were pointing towards the road. This was a strange coincidence, but there it was; a big, black SUV! As I watched the vehicle roll up to the stop sign, I had to laugh. I called back to the girls, "Real scary! It's a lady with a car seat and kids in the back!"

The highlight of our visit was the "Devil Tree." I had to park on the road to take photos as there was no shoulder there. This was the scariest part of the visit, as I envisioned some local flying around the corner and running me down as I tried to take photos.

We got back into the car and continued on the road, which dead-ended soon after the tree. The girls were disappointed that there was no cult house and that we hadn't been chased by a murderous driver, but they did think the tree was interesting.

Tree Spirits and Energy

The tree did get me thinking, though. Many people believe that some trees are inhabited by guardian spirits. The Ancient Greeks called these spirits dryads. A tree spirit is essentially the soul and guardian of the tree and they are disturbed and distressed by disrespect or damage to trees. Could a tree spirit, upset at the damage to this tree, be the cause of the uneasy feelings people have here?

Another theory is that if enough people visit a place and concentrate their energy on a particular idea, such as a lady in white on the stairs or a scream at midnight, it seems to create the phenomena. In other words, expectation leads to experience. If people expect the tree to radiate an aura of evil, might their imaginations fill in the blanks; especially on a dark, moonless night?

There is still the possibility of the ghosts of the murdered Johnston gang members. The feelings of dread that are experienced here could be due to lingering energy from the murders. Although the murder and burial site was not near this tree, if there are wandering spirits in the area, they would be attracted to this place where so many people come, hoping to catch a glimpse of the other side.

Left:
The trees grow away from the road because of power lines. Still, they provide quite the unusual and creepy sight.

Far left:
Cossart Road winds away towards the Devil Tree.

The mangled and abused Devil's Tree.

MIDNIGHT MARY - BRISTOL

Bordentown Road at night is dark and deserted. There is nothing there except big lakes joined by a bridge, a dock, and a clubhouse. At the end of the road is an industrial site and landfills. It is easy to see how someone driving alone would get spooked. I wasn't alone and I was hesitant to get out of the car.

We had driven up to Bordentown Road late on Halloween night to try and see the elusive creature known as Midnight Mary. Some drivers have seen a girl in a pink gown hitchhiking along this road. Other drivers have seen her gliding across the lake.

The background is the typical hitchhiking ghost story that has its roots in the 1930s and whose origins are unclear. Almost every geographic area in the U.S. has one of these hitchhiking young beauties. This particular one has been linked with Gertrude Spring, who is said to have been killed in a car accident on the way to her high school prom in 1935. Why is the ghost called Mary if her name is Gertrude?

Gertrude Spring

The 1930 U.S. Census reports two Gertrude Springs residing in Bristol. One was Gertrude M. Spring, who was 48 years old. The other was her daughter, Gertrude L. Spring, who was 20 years old. At 20 years old, she is too old to have been going to or from a prom. In 1935, she would have been 25 years old and was even less likely to have been going to or from a prom.

The December 15, 1932, *Doylestown Daily Intelligencer* reported that "Miss Gertrude Spring, Bristol, is confined to her home by illness."[4] She would have been 22 at the time. When I found this, I thought, *Aha! She died from the illness in 1935*. There was no further record of her in the censuses, so she either died or got married.

There was something more and I found it in the May 31, 1935 issue of the *New York Times*. According to an article there, on May 30, 1935 at 3 a.m. in the morning, Miss Gertrude Spring and a Mr. William Bagley, who was also 25 years old, were killed in an auto accident when his car ran off a sharp curve on Bristol Pike and struck a tree. Mr. Bagley was dead at the scene and Miss Spring died from her injuries an hour later at St. Francis Hospital in Trenton.

"Mr. Spring said his daughter and Mr. Bagley left Bristol …[on May 29]… for the Devon Horse Show… and planned to attend a dance in Philadelphia that night. They were on their way home when the accident occurred."[5] It is not clear exactly where on Bristol Pike the accident occurred, but it is clear that they did not go into a lake and it was not on Bordentown Road. Bordentown Road does begin near Bristol Pike in Levittown, but Gertrude didn't die there. It seems that the location of Bristol Pike together with the circumstances of her death in an auto accident returning from a dance and the date coinciding with the explosion of hitchhiker legends in the U.S., have combined to place Gertrude Spring in the wrong place (Manor Lake) as the wrong person; a hitchhiking ghost.

Time and retellings obscured the true facts of this story. Just when I had concluded that Midnight Mary was a legend that grew out of a tragedy, I started receiving reports of sightings of Midnight Mary.

More Reports

One pair of witnesses had parked and walked out on the dock . They couldn't see anyone, but they heard ballroom music coming from behind them. When they turned, they were confronted with a vision of Midnight Mary, gliding across the lake in her soaking wet, pink gown. One of the pair got scared and wanted to leave, but the other wanted to stay and see what would happen if they tried to get closer to the apparition. As they approached her on the bridge, she suddenly switched direction and began heading towards them. They ran for the car, but when she got within about five feet of them, she disappeared. They drove off, not wanting to see if she would come back.

Another account of Mary came from a security guard at the industrial park off New Ford Mill Road. A truck driver, who had a scheduled pickup at the plant, flew into the driveway by the guard station. When the security guard went out to see what was going on, the truck driver was upset and said he had to use the phone for an emergency. He had picked a hitch hiking girl on Bordentown Road who was soaking wet and kept saying she had to find Bobby. He was driving and trying his best to think of something to say to comfort her when suddenly, she was gone! All that was left was a puddle of water in the seat and a corsage left on the console of the cab.

The guard told him there was no sense calling the police because he had just met a local legend. He went on and told the driver that the water will dry, the flowers will disappear, and he would have a great story to tell. Sure enough, when they went to check the truck cab about ten minutes later to see the flowers, they were already gone. The puddle of water was still visible on the seat, but they didn't have a camera to take a photo. The truck driver was so shaken by the whole experience that he slept in the guard station.

So if Gertrude Spring is not Midnight Mary, who *is* Midnight Mary? Why does she walk down the road? If the above accounts are true, who is Bobby and why is she looking for him?

We headed out that Halloween night armed with these questions. Although we went up and down Bordentown Road, even stopping at the dock and getting out, we saw nothing except the deserted road, the lakes, and the piles of trash in the landfill. Is it possible that the ghostly lady seen on the road had something to do with the massive landfills that surrounded the lakes? Could it be an undiscovered murder victim dumped out there in the lake or the landfill? Whoever she is, she is definitely a very mysterious lady.

Bordentown Road and the huge landfill in the background.

Twin Tunnels - Downingtown

The Twin Tunnels are the one of the creepiest places I have ever been. After my first visit there, I remarked that if the Twin Tunnels are not haunted, then there is no place that is. As I drove up to the tunnels on a sunny day, I did not think that they looked spooky or haunted from the outside. They looked just like all the other railroad overpasses throughout the state.

But... as I drove through and reached the break between the twin tunnels, I was overcome by a terrible feeling of dread and doom, as if I were about to die.

As soon as I emerged from the darkness of the second tunnel on the other side, the feeling was gone.

That feeling of dread that I experienced is not unknown or even uncommon to me. I have come to associate it with residual energy. What this means is that something very traumatic occurred at a location and was somehow imprinted on the atmosphere or physical walls, floor, or even the ground under the place. When a person who is sensitive to these energies passes by, he or she is able to feel the emotion that has imprinted there.

My feeling as I returned home was that something very bad had happened in or around the tunnels. The feeling was so strong that I felt it was likely that several negative things had happened or were still happening there.

Research revealed very little in the way of history. There were no stories of train wrecks or unusual numbers of car accidents at the location. There were rumors of a suicide there, but the details were vague and varied from one telling to another, so this was likely more a legend than fact.

The only thing that I found related to the tunnels was that in 1995, the upper part of the body of an unidentified woman had been found by some hunters in the creek right next to the tunnels. Her legs were later found by a hiker in Bucks County, about fifty miles away. She is referred to as the "Suitcase Jane Doe." She has still never been identified and her murderer was never caught.

Is the overwhelming feeling of doom related to this unsolved murder? Time will tell as I feel that further exploration of the origin of this residual energy should be undertaken.

Looking into the darkness of the Twin Tunnels. From the outside, they weren't so scary... But, that wasn't the case on the inside...

Creepy Communities

Pennsylvania is full of old communities that have preserved their historical buildings so well that it almost seems as if you are stepping into the past as you walk down the sidewalks there. Buildings and homes give the passersby a glimpse of what life was like there in the 1700s, the Victorian Era, and even the 1940s. Is this why some towns and cities seem so haunted? Do the ghosts from the past linger because the scenery is so familiar? Some people theorize that this is so. Others believe that the high quartz content in the soil of some Pennsylvania areas make it easier for ghostly energy to manifest. Take a look at some of the creepy communities in Pennsylvania. What do you think?

Lansdowne

The Twentieth Century Club

I used to pass this place every day on the way to and from work. I admired the architecture and its designation as a historical place, but had never had the opportunity to go inside. I was not surprised when a friend of mine told me it was haunted. It just seemed to have that energy.

The story came from a plumber who had been called to do some emergency work there one night. He heard disembodied footsteps and the sounds of people talking in the building. Every time he went to check, thinking someone had walked in, he found that he was alone in the building. It got so bad that he called his wife to come and stay with him while he finished the job. He swore he would never again go into that building by himself.

I could find nothing in its history that would normally be associated with a haunting. The Twentieth Century Club was built in 1911 as a women's center for thought and action. The members of this club were interested in promoting science, literature, and art, and also helping the needy, especially children.

At least one of those women is still there. The disembodied voice of a woman has been heard from the balcony and a woman in a gray suit with her hair in a bun has been sighted in the library and walking towards the stairs.

We were fortunate enough to have the opportunity to investigate the building one evening in late autumn. As we entered the main auditorium, our attention was drawn to the balcony as there was a strong feeling of being watched from it. The presence was that of a woman, and although I did not get a clear picture of her in my mind, I did perceive that she was curious about us and what we were doing there.

Almost at the same time, I saw a shadow pass by the doorway to the left of the stage. We went to see what could have caused it, and as we went through the door, we experienced a heavy feeling in the air, like we were invading someone's space. At the top of the stairway, behind the door, I saw a shadow move through the room in front of me. Although I felt very

Twentieth Century Club's front entrance.
Shadows lurk behind these doors…

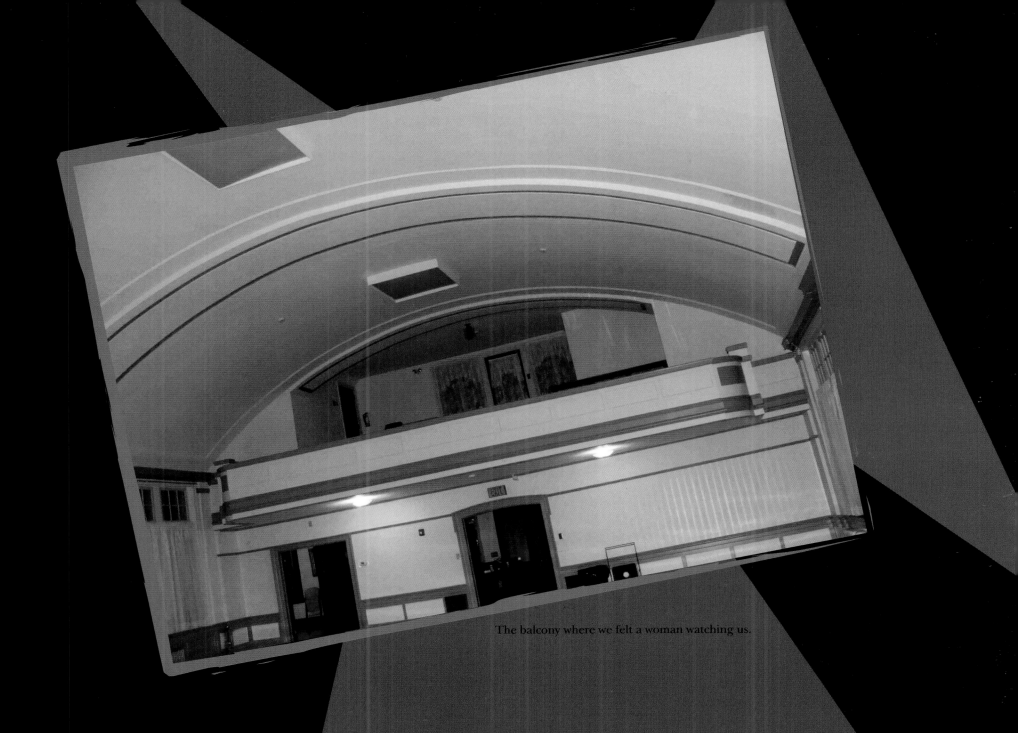

The balcony where we felt a woman watching us.

unwelcome there, I knew I had to go in and try to see what could have caused the shadow. When I got all the way across the room, I saw another doorway and then the shadow passed quickly right in front of me and into the doorway that led to the area behind the stage. I didn't want to upset whoever was back there, so I went back to the hallway to tell the others what I had seen. As I was beginning to tell them, one of the ladies from the borough called out, "I just saw a shadow pass through the doors at the back of the stage."

I was able to make contact with the spirit of a man in a suit. He indicated that he had lived nearby and attended many events there, so he liked to come down and see what was going on at the club. This corroborated our impressions that the spirits there were just curious about what people were doing and had good feelings toward the place.

Why did some people get frightened by things they saw there? I know from firsthand experience that seeing something or someone that you do not expect to see and that your mind knows cannot possibly be there is unnerving. Hearing footsteps come up behind you as you are trying to work and then turning to find an empty room can be upsetting as well. As we learn more about the resident spirits of the club, perhaps their presence won't be as unexpected to those who spend time there and everyone will see them for what we did; people who enjoyed spending time there so much in life they chose to continue to do so after death.

The Lansdowne Ghost

I first heard about this ghost when I lived in Lansdowne. I was talking to a friend of mine about local haunted places. He told me that there was one right near my neighborhood and it was in a public place; Providence Road! The spirit of a young girl haunted the area near the intersection of Lansdowne Avenue and Providence Road in Lansdowne. The story he heard was that a girl was walking home with her bike up the hill of Providence Road, coming towards Lansdowne Avenue when she was struck and killed by an automobile.

My inquiries about this resulted in my hearing the same story from other local people, but no one seemed to know the details of the accident or the approximate year in which this occurred.

According to the stories, if you drive down the road around midnight, you will see her walking with her bike. I drove up and down that road countless times at midnight, and after midnight, and I never saw anything unusual. The road is very steep and very dark at night, though, and it would be easy to be startled by someone walking along that road at night, so I thought there was nothing to this story—until one night in September.

It was about 10:45 p.m. and I was on my way home from a friend's house. I was stopped at a red light at the intersection of Lansdowne Avenue and Baily Road going towards Providence Road, which was at the next light. This is one of those intersections with the delayed green to allow people to turn, so I was waiting for my light to turn green and watching oncoming cars make their turns onto Baily Road.

That's when I noticed a woman standing in the middle of Lansdowne Avenue on the other side of the intersection. She was standing just on my side of the yellow line, facing my car. Her facial features were unclear, but I saw the outline of her hair, which looked like a puffy '80's 'do and her clothes, which were also absolutely 1980s. She was wearing acid-wash jeans, big socks pulled up over the bottom of her jeans, and white high top sneakers. I was struck by the fact that she was so perfectly 1980s. She was standing in the street, arms crossed over her stomach.

I started thinking, "Oh, great, this is just my luck. I want to go home, and there's some drunken woman standing in the road in the street, probably suicidal, and wants to jump in front of my car!" As I was thinking this and staring at her, she vanished. It was so odd; she was there, then she wasn't there. My mind still struggles to accept it, but I know what I saw.

When I told my friend about the weird experience I had on Lansdowne Avenue, he immediately said, "You saw the Lansdowne Ghost!" I don't know about that. It was a block away from the traditional spot, and what I saw was definitely a woman, not a girl. The intersection where I had that experience is at the edge of a hospital property and two blocks from a huge graveyard. As far as I am concerned, I still haven't seen the original Lansdowne Ghost, but I do think I saw a ghost.

Then I got an e-mail from a woman who had moved into a house near that intersection. She said that one night she was turning left onto Providence Road from Lansdowne Avenue and she slammed on her brakes to avoid hitting a woman who was standing in the middle of the road.

BAILY

LANDSDOWNE AVE D

SPEED 25

The woman was standing just to the right of the yellow line before disappearing.

The deadly intersection.

Shaken, she pulled into her driveway, got out of the car, and walked over to make sure the woman was all right. As she was trying to decide whether to be upset with herself for nearly hitting someone or upset with the woman for standing in the middle of the road at a dangerous intersection, she realized the woman was gone. She stood there for a few seconds in disbelief. It was impossible for the woman to have disappeared that quickly. There was nowhere for her to have gone without passing right by.

Still puzzled and thrown by the whole experience, she went back to her house and told her son she either wasn't getting enough sleep or she had just seen a ghost. The woman she saw also had big 1980s hair and big 1980s socks. She too had asked around the neighborhood and was told the same story I got about the girl with the bike and been confused since she saw a woman, not a girl, and this woman definitely didn't have a bike.

The friend who had originally told me the story swears that the story is true, as "everyone" heard it when they were growing up. When I asked him for an approximate date, he wasn't sure, but he seemed to think the accident happened at some time in the late 1960s or early 1970s. He didn't know anything about the woman we saw.

Just down Providence Road from the intersection is another intersection; Hilldale and Providence Roads. Since I first saw the woman, there were at least two serious accidents there. One of the accidents was fatal and involved a carload of teenagers. The other accident, although not fatal, resulted in serious injuries. It occurred when the driver of a fire truck, responding to a fire call, miscalculated the turn onto Providence and crashed through the wall that borders the road.

These two incidents show that this can be a dangerous area to drive in, so take extra care if you decide to go looking for the Lansdowne Ghost.

The Rock where the vanishing hitchhiker has been seen.

The Rock

Over the past few years I have received quite a few reports of a ghostly female hitchhiker right by the rock. She appears at night right by the rock. Drivers and passengers have reported that they are startled when they see her, but when they look back in the rearview mirror, she is gone.

I am not sure if this is a new ghost or if this is related to the stories of the Lansdowne Ghost. The people who I have interviewed claim to have seen her, though, there one minute, gone the next, in a standard "vanishing hitchhiker" manner.

First Presbyterian Church

People who have thought they were alone in this building have found that they are not. One man reported that he was in the men's room in the basement when he heard footsteps approach. When he came out, he saw that he was alone and he had not heard anyone leave. Others I have spoken to have reported feelings of being watched or the feeling that someone is behind them while in the basement.

Why would a church be haunted? This was a question I had asked myself many times. The solution came to me suddenly one day when listening to an EVP recorded near the site of an old camp meeting. I asked why the spirit of the man who haunted the place was there and the response was, "He's damned." A spirit who felt that he was a sinner in need of redemption may look for help before crossing over into the spirit world; perhaps spirits are looking for a way to unburden their souls or gain help in seeing the way to the light. A logical place to look for that kind of help would be in a church. If one is looking for a peaceful place to sit and think and pray for guidance, a church would be a good place to go.

In addition, people who volunteer and work at churches often devote their lives to the place. It is possible that so much of their energy is connected to and centered on the church, they gave their life's work to that, and they don't want to leave, so they choose to continue watching over the place.

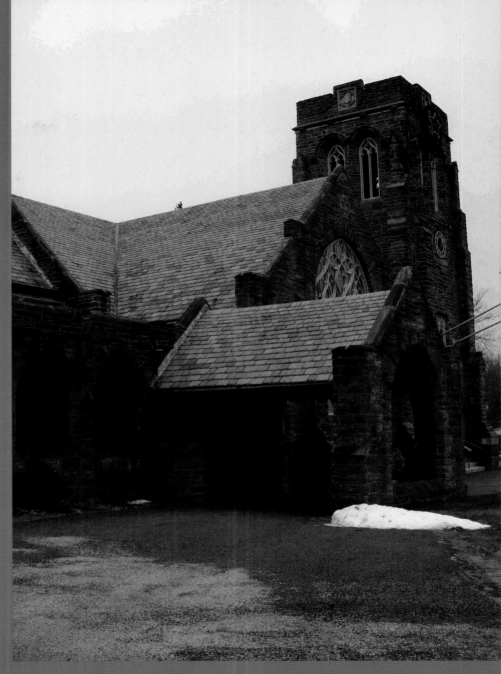

The Haunted Church.

Darby

Anne's Rock

This is another of those legendary places that everyone "knows" is haunted. We were led there on a freezing cold day by a local woman who recounted the legend for us. The most popular legend is that rock is haunted by a Lenape princess named Anne who was having an affair with an English man. The rock was their meeting place. They were caught by her father and she climbed to the top of the rock and jumped off, committing suicide when she realized they were not going to be allowed to be together.

Another legend holds that Anne was struck by lightning and killed as she waited on the rock. The outline of her form is said to be burned into the rock. I didn't see a burned figure, but I did see a painted figure on the rock.

The creek was frozen in most places and it was about fifteen degrees below zero that day with the wind chill, but as I stood at the edge of the boulder and looked down into the creek I had the overwhelming urge to go into the water. Upon playback of our audio from the rock, one male voice came through very clear. It said, "I want you…in the water."

The rock is left behind from an Ice Age glacier that passed through. Just being in the presence of such a massive boulder that was left behind by an even more massive glacier so long ago is enough to give one something to think about. It would be a great place to connect with the Earth, if it weren't for that uneasy feeling of being watched and that seductive voice urging others to join him in the water.

There aren't a lot of clues in history as far as who Annie was and how she became associated with the rock. In 1900, it was part of the Tribble family farm and there is a nice photo of them in front of the rock in Lindy Wardell's book, *Darby Borough*. In the photo, the rock is actually two large boulders, one on top of the other. At some point the top rock must have fallen, leaving only the bottom one jutting out over the water.

Anne's Rock where you may be lured to a watery grave…

Boone's Tunnel

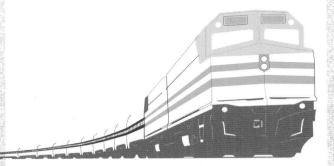

I had heard all kinds of rumors about the "Mummy's Tunnel" or "The Devil's Road" in Darby. I had never been there, so when friend and fellow investigator, Carol, who grew up in the neighborhood where the tunnel is located, offered to take me there, I jumped at the chance. The day that Carol, our lead investigator Lori Clark, and I picked to go was described on the weather report as the coldest day of the year; and as we headed off towards the tracks under Pine Street, we looked like we were on an arctic expedition.

When we got onto the tracks, the tunnel was right there, less than a quarter mile down from where we were standing. It looked dark and spooky, even in broad daylight.

Carol turned to me and said, "Well, there it is. Do you feel anything?"

I paused and tried to focus on what, if anything was going on at the tracks and the tunnel.

Immediately, I picked up that there were three deaths on the tracks near where we were standing. I felt that all were young men and that one was a suicide, one was an accident, and one was thought to be a suicide, but was really a murder. When I told Carol this, she said that there were at least three deaths that she knew of. She confirmed that one was a suicide who had been seen just sitting on the tracks, talking to the air, ignoring the approaching CSX train. The circumstances of the others she knew about were less clear cut. She said that in one of the instances, the person had fallen asleep on the tracks. It was unclear whether this was a suicide or not. She also said that she knew two of the people killed there were men and the third she was not sure about.

At this point I was not sure whether we should go down through the tunnel. If the ghosts were of suicides and murder victims, the entities that remained there could potentially be pretty volatile. Carol assured me that the ghosts in the tunnel were not dangerous or aggressive, so I agreed to go.

As we walked toward the tunnel, she said that people who walk down the tracks in this area avoid walking through the tunnel. They will walk up the hill, around the tunnel on the top and then continue on the tracks on the other side. According to Carol, though, avoiding the tunnel doesn't mean you will avoid the ghosts. Many people over the years have reported seeing a man in a gray uniform approach on the opposite side of the tracks, walk past them, and then disappear when they turn to get a better look at him.

When you first enter the tunnel, it is not so bad. As you go farther, though, it gets darker and darker. Your footsteps and any sounds echo back at you in a disorienting way. Legend has it that a train full of passengers was traveling at top speed and was too high for the tunnel. As it hit the tunnel, the train was torn apart and numerous passengers were stuck in the wreckage. Many of them died. I could find no record of a train crash, but according to the *Darby Borough* book by the Darby Borough Historical and Preservation Society, "crashes involving trains and cars have occurred at the tunnel over the years."[6]

...And the Train Cometh...With a Bang

As we went further into the darkness, I became concerned about the possibility of a train coming while we were in the tunnel. Carol assured us that the trains that use these tracks are very slow and we would have lots of warning with plenty of time to get out of the tunnel. Reassured, we continued through the darkness.

We walked all the way through the tunnel to the other side and then decided to go back towards the center to have a communication session. As we stood next to the tracks, looking at our recorders, we heard a loud bang off to our left. It sounded like someone threw something against the side of the tunnel.

We looked to where the sound came from, but there was nothing there. Then Lori said, "Is that the train?"

It was a train and it was coming quickly towards us down the track. There was no time to ask what happened to the slow freight train. We had to run. So there we were, running towards the end of the tunnel, carrying all of our equipment and weighted down with our layers of clothing we had worn against the cold.

As you can probably surmise, we made it out in time because I am here writing this, but it was an upsetting experience. If you decide to venture into Boone's Tunnel, don't forget to watch the tracks.

When we reviewed the audio from that day, we could hear the loud bang that caught our attention. I wondered what caused it, since we were alone in the tunnel. I also wonder what would have happened if we hadn't heard the bang. Would we have been able to get out of the tunnel in time? I don't know. I do know this; I am grateful to whoever made the noise.

Boone's Tunnel—listen for the train, or else…

Darby Free Library

This library is America's oldest public library, formed in 1743 by a group of local Quakers who felt a lending library was essential for their growing community. The library building was built in 1872 with funds raised by members and friends. It was always a library, even though the building resembles a church.

It is unclear who or what haunts the library, but many of the people who spend time there have witnessed books inexplicably falling off the shelves. Others who have done research there have felt someone come up behind them and tap them on the shoulder. When they turn around, no one is there.

The area where the research room is, connects to what was once the living quarters of the librarian. It is now a storage area. The theories about the identity of the ghost are that it may be one of the resident librarians still watching over the place or it could be a spirit that was attached to the land that was there before the library was built and is making its presence known.

Darby Free Library
1001 Main Street
Darby, PA 19023
610-586-7310
www.darbylibrary.org

The Darby Library resembles a church, but ghosts still like to take books from the shelves.

The Historic Blue Bell Tavern where a British soldier may still haunt.

Blue Bell Tavern

This site is registered as an official historical site, and with good reason! It was built around 1766, according to records, although it may have been there earlier as a tavern to serve traffic going to and from Philadelphia on the south side of the city. George Washington was first welcomed to Philadelphia here, and it is also the site of his farewell speech. This shows how important a part of colonial life this meeting place was.

The grounds around the inn were the site of skirmishes during the British occupation of Philadelphia. One of these skirmishes is said to be the source of the haunting.

The battle was in November of 1777, and broke out right in front of the inn. Five colonial soldiers were killed, and one British soldier fell, dying, in the road. As he died, he reportedly uttered something to the effect of, "Now I will never leave here." According to some past residents and visitors, he has kept his word and makes his presence known by fooling with electrical appliances. He also plays tricks on people by stealing small objects, hiding them, and later returning them. One lucky resident reported actually seeing the trousers and boots of a soldier, with the rest of the figure in a mist.

A lifelong resident of Darby and local history expert that I spoke with, Betty Schell, related a frightening occurrence at the Blue Bell. Back in the 1940s, when she was child, a group of neighborhood children often played in and around the old inn. One day, during a game of Cowboys and Indians, they decided to hang one of the boys. They really did hang him inside the inn, and tragically, he died. The playful nature of the paranormal activity at the inn makes me wonder if he ever left.

Blue Bell Tavern
7303 Woodland Avenue
Philadelphia, PA 19142

Old Chester

Third Street Bridge

During the time I lived in the Sun Hill section of Chester I heard many stories about locations in and around the old section of the city that were "haunted." One of these places was the Third Street Bridge. Since this was not close to our neighborhood and was outside the old section, I never had the chance to go there until recently.

We were on a walking tour of Old Chester and were on our way down to see the marker at the spot where William Penn landed when a great friend and fellow paranormal investigator, Diane, pointed the bridge out to me. On our way back from the Penn landing spot, I took a few minutes to stop. I didn't know the whole story at that time, just that there had been some kind of disaster there.

I was expecting to pick up on screams and the terror I normally experience. What I got was a young boy calling for help. He seemed to be in the water, trying to stay above. I asked Diane about the bridge collapse and she said it had something to do with a boat going under the bridge and a bunch of people watching from the bridge, which then collapsed under their weight. She said she had not been over there to investigate yet, but she was sure she would get something. I wondered if a little boy ever drowned there.

The restored Third Street Bridge. Does a boy's spirit still call for help?

In a newspaper article from 1951 I found the whole story of the bridge collapse which happened on September 10, 1921 and killed at least twenty-four people. The most interesting part of the article was the event that caused the crowd to gather on the bridge. They gathered to watch attempts of rescue workers to recover the body of a five-year-old boy who had fallen into the river and drowned. The river they refer to is the Chester River, which we now call Chester Creek.

The weight of the crowd proved to be too much for the bridge, which had been damaged when a coal barge hit the foundation back in 1909. Although some people had felt a vibration in the bridge, they were too interested in the rescue to give up their spot. The main part of the bridge was still intact and is there today. The footpath portion was the section that had collapsed.

Why did I see the spirit of one boy when at least twenty men, women, and children drowned there that day? Since I didn't interact with him, all I could do was guess. One of the articles stated that accounts of how the little boy fell into the river were at odds. Some of the witnesses, all of whom seem to have been other children, stated that he fell in while watching other boys swim. Others said that the boy had taken a rowboat onto the river and it began to leak and he went under with it.

I am not sure if what I saw that day was the boy's spirit, crying out for help or just an imprint of a traumatic event from the past. Whatever it was that I saw, it showed me that the Third Street Bridge is haunted by its past.

Intersection of Edgmont and Providence Roads

When Chester was the center of government for the county, executions took place at the gallows on the point formed by Providence and Edgmont Avenues. This is now the parking lot for the Edgmont Diner. Legend has it that no plants will grow there. The photo shows that there are hedges around the restaurant, which sort of nixes that legend. Although plants do grow there, it is an eerie place, especially in the early morning hours. Over the years, there have been reports of shadowy figures lurking in the area.

Colonial law stated that executed criminals had to be buried within a certain distance of the execution. Tradition requires their burial at a crossroads. Those executed at this gallows were buried in the slaves' cemetery, which was on Edgmont Avenue above Twelfth Street.

After several criminals were executed and buried there, the locals began to shun the burial ground and the cross-roads as a haunted or cursed place. As time passed, the place became overgrown and the fact that it was a burial ground was forgotten.

In 1868, two brothers commenced the building of a row of homes on the east side of Edgmont, above Twelfth. While they were digging the cellars, a number of human bones were unearthed. They assumed these were the bones of Native Americans, since there was no memory of there being an old graveyard there. It is unclear what happened to those remains.

This crossroads was the site of the colonial gallows.

The Galloping Ghost of William Wilson

This ghost is a result of an unjust execution carried out at Gallows Hill in old Chester. The ghost is not of the person who was hanged, but of the brother who tried to save her. The unfortunate woman who was executed was an unlucky victim of her own bad choices and the society in which she lived.

There were relatively few executions by hanging in colonial and early Pennsylvania because the Quakers, who were the primary English settlers here, were opposed to the death penalty. Public executions in the colonies and other parts of the western world in the eighteenth and early nineteenth centuries were viewed by some as a moral lesson for citizens. They were one of the few forms of public entertainment available at the time outside of church-related offerings. I tend towards the feeling that these executions were more entertaining for Americans than they were educational.

The road leading to the courthouse. A galloping horse and rider is still seen and heard here.

Elizabeth Wilson

Hangings were rare, and hangings of women rarer still. Huge crowds turned out for these spectacles. January 3rd of 1786 was no exception. The day was bitterly cold, but that didn't stop a crowd from gathering to watch Elizabeth Wilson be hanged. She had been sentenced to death for the murder of her illegitimate infant twin sons.

Elizabeth spoke not one word in her defense during the trial, so we are unsure of what occurred from the time she left her home with the two infants to the time she returned home alone, disheveled, and incoherent some days later. The bodies of the two infants were discovered some time later in a wooded area; some accounts place this area not far from her home in East Bradford Township, Pennsylvania, and others place this location in Newtown Square. She had ridden with a neighbor to Newtown Square, where she was supposed to be meeting the father of the children to get married.

Her lack of response to the charges against her resulted in her conviction, even though the evidence was circumstantial. Unfortunately for Elizabeth, they did not need to prove that she murdered her children; all they needed to do was prove that she had concealed their deaths. Pennsylvania had enacted a law in 1781 that made "the concealment of the death of a bastard child conclusive evidence to convict the mother of murder."[7] Her lack of communication meant that she concealed their deaths. Missing from the proceedings was the father of the children. Elizabeth's brother, William, arrived after she was convicted and sentenced and he was able to get her to tell the story. Her version implicated the absent father in the deaths.

William did some investigating and tracked down the father and took his evidence of the father's deception to the Supreme Executive Council. They were granted a stay of execution from them just hours before the execution was scheduled to be carried out. According to newspaper accounts of the day, William traveled through hell and high water when his horse drowned in his attempt to cross the icy Schuylkill River and he was forced to swim the river and find another horse to continue his journey.

William arrived minutes after his sister was dead. To this day, people have reported the sound of horse's hooves galloping up Fourth Street to the old Chester Jail. The sound is usually accompanied by a shadowy horse and rider who stop when they reach the site of the old Jail.

Schools, Clubs, and Caco-Demons

The building on Fifth Street had been many different things over the years; a fire house, an Italian-American Club, and a private club. One of my friends was a bartender there when it was a private club and she told me about various things that she and others had witnessed. She had seen a large shadowy figure going down the stairs and a man in old-fashioned clothing in the bar. One patron had seen a woman in a long white dress gliding across the floor. Another patron had seen an old woman in black in the mirror of the restroom. Others reported extreme cold spots and the uncomfortable feeling of being watched. There were issues with electronic devices and everyone seemed to feel the place was haunted. They thought it may have been from when it was a firehouse and asked me to come over sometime and give my impressions.

During a walkthrough of the building, I noticed one room seemed unusually cold and charged with energy. I was told this was the employees break room. The energy also seemed concentrated in one area that looked like a closet, which had, at one time been the top of a stairway to the basement.

The basement itself was very uncomfortable for me. The feeling of being watched was overwhelming. They said that they had originally had another bar area in the basement, but decided to close it because no one seemed to want to stay down there. I did not get a clear picture of what was there, just that the feeling of negativity was overwhelming.

In doing some research years later, I ran across an interesting tidbit in a *History of Delaware County* by Ashmead. Apparently lore among the students of the old school at 5th and Welsh Streets, less than a block from this place, told of a Caco-demon that lived in the basement!

According to *The Encyclopedia of the Occult* by Lewis Spence, a Caco-demon is a type of evil spirit that changes form so no one knows what it looks like. Had this entity relocated when the school house was torn down? This would explain the varied forms that had been seen as well as the negativity I felt.

The place has changed ownership a few times since then and gone through several renovations. Last time I checked it was a private gentleman's club. I wonder what the Caco-demon thinks of that!

The House on Sun Hill

Sun Hill was built in the early 1900s to house the management employees of Sun Shipbuilding. Our house was built in 1940 and was owned by the same family until 1978, when it was purchased by the Campbells. They lived there until 1984, when Mr. Campbell was killed crossing I-95. The house was then purchased by a couple. The wife refused to live there, so six months later, it was sold to my mother.

My mother had been desperate to find a place to live as we had been given very short notice to move out of our rented home. When she found this place at such a good price, she didn't hesitate and we moved right in. There were indicators that something was wrong from the first day.

One of my mother's friends who was helping us move in announced that the house was haunted. She swore that she had heard someone coming up the stairs while she was in the bathroom. I had forgotten about this until later that night when I heard someone coming up the stairs. Not accustomed to having my own room, I had left the door open. There were only two other people in the house with me, my mother and my sister. They were both in bed.

I held my breath and tried to stay still as I waited for what I assumed to be an intruder approach my door. I heard the footsteps pass my door, but saw nothing, not even a shadow. A few seconds later, I heard a door open and my sister's face peered around the door jamb. "Can I sleep in here with you?" she asked, "I keep hearing weird noises."

This became the norm from then on. Every night we would lie awake, waiting for the footsteps. They only came up once a night. After that we could sleep. Eventually, we didn't even notice it anymore.

What we did notice was that it was impossible to take a bath or shower when we were alone in the house. Every time we tried to do this, we would hear footsteps slowly come up the stairs and stop at the door. The footsteps were so unnerving and threatening we just stopped taking baths or showers unless someone else was home. In addition to the footsteps, we noticed that utensils mysteriously disappeared from the kitchen. Ice cream scoops seemed to be a favorite choice for this. They would later turn up in the oddest places, like under sofa cushions or on top of our clothes in dresser drawers. Scissors, tape, postage stamps, hammers, and screwdrivers all were similarly targeted. Of course, these disappearances would often result in heated arguments among us as we each accused each other of taking the items.

In looking back, I find it interesting how we and many others I have talked to since arrange their routines to accommodate invisible others they share their homes with. We figured the "night walker" as we called him was probably Mr. Campbell, who had been killed on his way home. Maybe he was still checking on the family as he had done in life.

We never found out who it was who came up the stairs if we were alone in the bath or shower or who was stealing the tools and utensils. Our attempts to resolve the situation by helping the ghost to move on were unsuccessful and after every attempt, we were subjected to an escalation in activity. After one attempt at talking the ghost into leaving, I and two of my friends were relaxing on the sofa and reflecting on what we had done when we observed a side chair rise about two feet off the floor and then crash down. Next we tried a sage cleansing and the following morning I woke up to find all of the downstairs area rugs completely soaked and dripping wet. We never did figure out what the source of that water was and I started to think the ghost was showing us he wasn't going anywhere.

Eventually, we moved and rented the house out. Although we never told the tenants what we experienced there, they all have reported events similar to what we experienced.

New Hope

The Mill House

This average-looking home was the scene of one of the saddest stories I've heard on the New Hope Ghost Tour. During the time when the mill was running, this house was the home of a foreman. He was a widower with a beautiful daughter who met and ultimately fell in love with one of the mill workers.

She and the young man began to meet in secret and eventually she became pregnant. No one knows when her father discovered her secret, but suddenly, no one saw the girl anymore. Her sweetheart waited for her to contact him, and wondered what had happened.

One bitterly cold night, neighbors were awakened by screaming from the girl's house. Remember, no one at the time knew of her condition. Suddenly, the screaming stopped. No more was heard from the house at 63 Ferry Street. The next morning, the house was shut tight, the foreman and his daughter gone. One older woman talked to her neighbor about that night. She had sworn that after the screaming ended, she heard the thin wail of an infant. How much of this is fact and how much is legend?

One thing is for sure. During the sixties, the back field, where the outhouses were once located, was excavated. The remains of a newborn infant were found in the area behind that mill house. In addition, many people walking Ferry Street on cold winter nights have heard the crying of a young girl, and the crying of an infant. Some people even claimed to have seen the glowing figure of a girl in the area behind 63 Ferry Street. Perhaps someday she will be reunited with the baby she lost so long ago.

I myself walked down Ferry Street towards the river one very cold November night a few years ago. As I passed the end of that row of homes, something made me stop. The hair on the back of my neck stood up and I shivered in air that suddenly became even colder. I was sure that if I had turned around at that moment, I would have seen the ghostly girl of Ferry Street, but suddenly I didn't want to. A feeling of complete despair came over me and all I wanted to do was go home. I did not turn around. I wonder what I would have seen if I had.

This mill house was a scene of a tragic drama.

The Inn at Phillips Mill

This Inn has a great reputation for their excellent cuisine and has been rated by the *CityPaper* of Philadelphia as one of the top ten places to dine outside. It is also listed on many directories of haunted places. The ghost of a woman in a long, high-collared gown is said to haunt the stairway and upstairs hall. Her presence is often felt as she brushes against guests as they ascend and descend the staircase or walk the hall. A ghost has also been reported associated with a rocking chair at the inn. It is unclear whether there are two ghosts, or if this is the same female ghost. I have also been unable to locate the origin of the ghost.

While dining at the Inn of Phillips Mill near New Hope, Pennsylvania, I asked our waitress if she ever saw the ghost. She said, in a very serious voice, "No, but one night I was taking food to one of the guest rooms, and on the back stairway I saw a little white dog. And we have no dogs at this restaurant." With that, she turned and left our table.

Inn at Phillips Mill
2590 River Road
New Hope, PA 18938
215-862-9919
www.theinnatphillipsmill.com

Parry Mansion

Benjamin Parry arrived in Coryell's Ferry in 1781. He was 24 years old and couldn't wait to get started in business. He soon owned mills on both sides of the river. When a fire destroyed several of the mills, Parry rebuilt and called his mill New Hope. The town soon changed from Coryell's Ferry to New Hope.

He built this mansion in the center of town in 1784 and lived in it for fifty-five years until his death. The next four generations lived in the home until 1966 when it was sold to the New Hope Historical Society.

The house, once filled with family, is now filled with period furniture, or so it seems. We are not sure who it is that lingers in the mansion, but visitors and docents have reported seeing a woman in a Victorian-era, black-beaded dress in the Victorian bedroom. Other visitors have heard the sound of children's footsteps and laughter ringing through the halls.

My experience was in the Victorian bedroom – a very sick girl, ill with some kind of painful illness that drove her mad, was tied to the bed. She was sitting up, arms spread at her sides, and she was crying. Many generations of the Parry family lived in the house and all of the furniture in the museum belonged to the families that lived there.

Parry Mansion remains
one of the showplaces
of New Hope.

The Victorian Bed where I saw
a young girl confined due to a
painful illness.

Van Sant House

Former Ichabod Wilkinson House, this is the earliest existing house in New Hope. Ichabod Wilkinson was a mill owner from Rhode Island, and when one of his daughters married a Van Sant, their name stuck to the house.

People have reported seeing the apparition of a man with a noose around his neck hanging from the roof joist. He was first reported by workmen who were renovating the house. After the renovations, many visitors to the shop that occupied the building reported being touched near the face or shoulders in the area where the hanged man was seen. Eerily, the feet of the hanged man would be about where the head and shoulders of a person standing on the floor would be. Were these people feeling the feet of the man hanging from the rafters?

One night as I was walking by the house, I saw that it was unoccupied and up for sale. I took the opportunity to walk over for a closer look and I saw a woman walk through one of the rooms. I backed up quickly, thinking I had been mistaken and that there was someone living there. Later that evening, I made sure to go by the Van Sant House again. It was dark and empty. There was no sign of anyone having been inside recently, either.

I did some research into the history and found that a previous owner that had operated a store called Majik Horse had often seen the spirit of a woman by the fireplace. Many people reported feeling cold and threatened by this presence. The brother of the proprietor of Majik Horse swore he was attacked by the ghost one night.

He said he had entered the room when he was suddenly struck by a wall of frigid air and overcome by fear. Then he saw someone coming for his throat out of the fireplace. He ran from the room, followed by an icy wind that blew a heavy tapestry off the wall. Was this the woman? The woman I saw did not seem threatening or scary at all, so this may have been the spirit of the hanged man or perhaps even another yet unknown inhabitant of the old house.

The last time I was in New Hope I saw that the house had been sold. I wonder what the new residents will experience.

Who is the colonial-era woman seen walking in the Van Sant House?

Pickett House

Joseph Pickett was a painter who operated a grocery and butcher shop here on Mechanic Street. He painted in his free time.

About twenty-five years after Joseph Pickett died, people that occupied the property reported the sound of heavy footsteps climbing the exterior staircase. Problem was, the staircase was no longer there.

The residents also reported seeing the apparition of Pickett sitting at the bottom of the bed in what was once the artist's bedroom. They also heard shutters banging, had chalk writing mysteriously appear on the wall, and were awakened by persistent knocking at the door in the middle of the night. There was never anyone there.

Pickett seems to enjoy having his presence known. One night he followed Adele Gamble around as she led a ghost tour down Mechanic Street. She didn't know he was there, but after the tour some attendees asked her who the man was that followed her around all night. She asked them to describe him and the description matched Pickett exactly.

Once the home of artist Joseph Pickett.

Wedgwood Inn

The first story that I heard about this place was that the ghost of Joseph Pickett could be seen on the grounds behind the inn, hard at work on one of his paintings. He did paint a picture from there; it now hangs in the Museum of Modern Art.

The first hand reports were not of Pickett. Instead, young female visitors to the inn reported encountering the ghost of a young girl name Sarah, who described herself as a slave. She and her family had become separated as they traveled the Underground Railroad and she was looking for them. Other guests at the inn had reported scratching sounds by the former servants' stairs.

During renovations, a secret room was found under the porch floor. First, a perfectly two-foot square rock was discovered. When it was lifted, they saw a wooden hatch door. It opened into a hand-hewn stone room.

Inside the inn, while removing the old servants staircase, which led from the kitchen to the room above it, they found a second landing which had created a hidden space. So, at one time a person could have come down the servant's stairs and through a storage room into the underground room. The Wedgwood House was known to be part of the Underground Railroad, a secret network designed to help enslaved Africans in the south escape to freedom in the North.

So why is this in the "1870" Wedgwood Inn? Wasn't the Civil War over by then? The current Wedgwood Inn was built in 1870, but it was built on the foundation of an older, circa 1720 building known as the Hip-Roof House. Washington and his troops camped in the area on December of 1776, up to the night they made the Christmas Eve crossing of the Delaware River. It is thought that the stone room had been constructed during the Revolution as a place to store and hide ammunition and/or supplies. It is possible someone later saw this room as the perfect hiding place for escaping slaves.

The Wedgwood's pleasant exterior hides a secret underground room.

Van Sant Bridge

This is one of twelve covered spans preserved in Bucks County and has generated more ghost stories than any other covered bridge in the area.

Crybaby Bridge

One story associated with it is the "Crybaby Bridge" Legend that seems to exist in every area of the country. A young unmarried girl, who is either pregnant or has the newborn, is thrown out of her home, abandoned by her lover, and decides to end it all by throwing herself and her baby off the bridge. The story goes that if you stand on the bridge and look over the side, you can hear a baby crying. Well, the bridge is about three feet above the water, so the chances of anyone committing suicide with a leap from it are highly unlikely.

A Hanged Man

The other story associated with the bridge is that there is the shape of a man hanging from the beams of the bridge. Supposedly horse thieves were hanged from the bridge. The problem with this is that there is no record of anyone being hanged on the inside of a bridge in Pennsylvania. It was customary to hang them from a gallows at a crossroads. There may have been an unrecorded lynching, but again, it is unlikely they would have been hanged from the beams of the bridge as this would make travel through the bridge very difficult.

Inside the Van Sant bridge.

Activity Persists

Still, the reports of activity there persist. It could be a case of high expectation leading to over reaction to natural events or it could be that there is something there and these legends grew up to try and explain the presences on the bridge.

Many people who have visited the bridge at night have reported being pushed and have experienced equipment failure and sudden feelings of anger towards the people they are with. My feeling of the origin of the haunting is based on impressions that I have from there; I have found no historical evidence to back this up. I feel that there were two thieves that would sit in the top beams and jump down to hijack and rob wagons as they passed through. This could explain the feelings of aggression that some people have had, as well as the images of men up in the rafters. It could even explain the crying sounds. These could be the residual cries of a victim or victims of robbery.

A mystery area forms as Rich Hickman takes readings in the Van Sant Bridge.

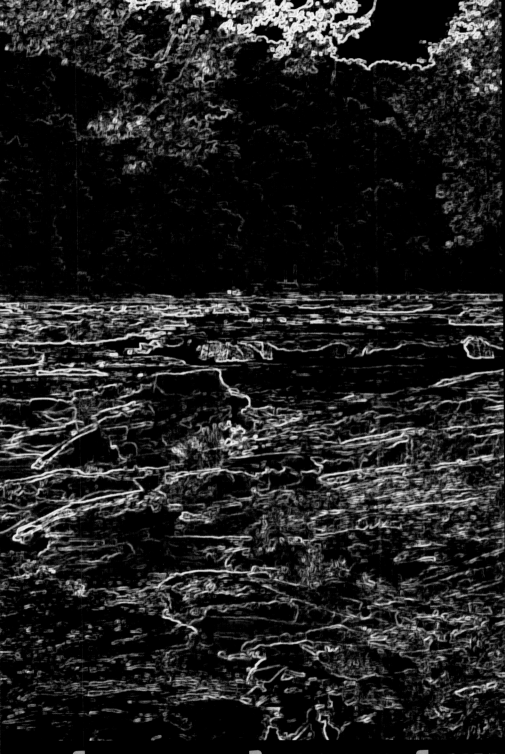

Spooksylvania

Travel a short distance from the big cities of Pennsylvania and it will become apparent that most of Pennsylvania is very rural. There are many wild areas where there are no people or signs of civilization for miles. Pennsylvania has lonely mountains, wild forests, and acres and acres of parkland. Some of these places are not as uninhabited as they seem at first glance. Over the years, explorers, hunters, and hikers have all reported experiencing the unmistakable presence of something supernatural as they explored an area where they assumed they would be alone.

Beautiful Ohiopyle Park was the scene of a troubling disappearance.

Betty Knox - Ohiopyle

Beautiful Betty Knox was born in 1842 in Fayette County, Pennsylvania, and lived in what is now part of Ohiopyle State Park. She was said to have possessed a flawless and unearthly beauty. Her mother died when she was a toddler and she lost her father when she was a teenager. The local men thought that since she was alone, now she would marry one of them, but she turned down every one of their offers. She lived a solitary life, working hard to survive every day.

It is hard to believe today, but this young lady walked twenty-five miles every day during harvest season, with her ox, hauling grain to the mill for the far-flung farms of the area. She then returned flour to them on her way back home. She became a fixture in the existence of the residents there. Everyone probably knew Betty and her route. Perhaps this was her undoing.

A Soldier Arrives

It is said that in the fall of 1862, when Betty was walking her route, she came across a young man, lying half-dead in the woods. He was a Union Army deserter who was wounded and ill. Something about him touched Betty because she brought him back to her home and tried to nurse him back to health. Unfortunately, he was too far gone and he died. She buried him next to her father, in an unmarked grave near her cabin.

Betty changed after his death. Local men thought for sure she would give one of them a chance now, but her heart was broken when the soldier died. She didn't talk to anyone, only speaking the words necessary to conduct her business. Most people admired her work ethic, but there must have been someone who harbored some secret resentment against her. Were they threatened by this independent woman's free spirit? Maybe one of her spurned suitors just couldn't get over the rejection. We will never know what really happened in those isolated hills.

It was late summer 1878 and the locals thought it was odd that they hadn't seen Betty and her ox for a few days. When grain began to pile up in her customer's barns as the harvests came in, concern grew that she had become ill and was in need of help. Independent or no, they decided to check on her. They arrived at her cabin and found it deserted. Her ox was gone, too.

Fearing that she had been attacked or injured along her route, the locals formed search parties and scoured the entire area. No evidence of Betty or the ox was found. Winter came and went with no sign of Betty or her ox. The next spring, just when people began to think that maybe she had picked up and left, some local children made a horrifying discovery.

A Morbid Discovery

The bones of an ox were found chained to a tree near one of the springs on Betty's route. Betty had never used a chain on her ox, but the remains of the leather halter that was found with the bones bore Betty's mark. This area had been searched several times when it was first noticed that she had disappeared, and the ox had not been there. The bones found that spring were described as having the appearance of having been there all winter.

Where did she go and what happened to her? Hunters and fishermen have reported seeing the pale form of a woman through the trees. She is as elusive in death as she was in life, always staying just out of reach or range of binoculars.

If her ox had never been found, I would likely agree with the locals who thought she up and left. When the ox was found chained to a tree, it indicated to me that some person had been involved in her disappearance. Betty didn't use a chain on her ox and certainly wouldn't have chained her ox to a tree to starve to death. If she were leaving, she would have taken the ox with her or sold it to raise money.

Could she have been attacked by an animal and her remains scattered? Then again, there was the ox. Mountain lions and bears don't chain oxen to trees and anyone who found the ox would have brought it to town or the nearest farm rather than chain it to a tree – unless there was some reason for leaving it there.

Betty's route and routine was well-known. She traveled the same route every day. When I visited the park and the area around it, it was not hard to imagine someone following her, memorizing her route, and waiting for the opportunity to strike. Whatever happened, whether she was killed because she fought back or killed accidentally in an effort to subdue her, there is one thing I am certain of. She is buried somewhere in the woods along her route.

A Serial Killer?

As I walked the paths near where her ghost has been reported, I began to get a picture of Ted Bundy in my mind. It bothered me for days afterward. I thought this must be a mistake. A serial killer would not have gone unnoticed in late nineteenth century Fayette County. I found no record of unexplained disappearances of women in the area. I was thinking it was unrelated until I began writing up the story. Ted Bundy popped into my head again as I recounted the section about the Union soldier.

That's it! I thought. Some person must have pretended to be injured, knowing that she would try and help him. He may even have let her take him back to her cabin to get her to a place where he knew they would be alone and isolated. He would have had uninterrupted time to clean up any signs of a struggle since she lived alone. Her attacker was someone who had a place to hide the ox. Perhaps he planned to try and get rid of it, but when there was so much interest in her disappearance he simply chained it to a tree, assuming it would be found before winter, but it wasn't...

Next time you are out by Ohiopyle Park on a still and clear night, turn right at the Game Commission Shed onto the dirt road that bears right for less than 1/8 mile. Turn off your car engine and lights and look carefully. You may see her pale shade.

Chique's or Chickie's Rock - Lancaster

My first visit to this place was in 1999 with a friend of mine who had taken me to many haunted outdoor locations in Pennsylvania. He was in the Navy Reserves and had worked as a hunting guide in Pennsylvania and also as a trail guide in Colorado. He knew his way around the woods and was not a jumpy person. I, on the other hand, am not an experienced hiker and tend to get nervous around wild animals. I would rather face a ghost than a rabid raccoon any day.

He didn't tell me where we were going until we got there. From the car, it didn't look like much. He promised there was a trail down to a very nice view of the river. The trail was easy and it wasn't dark yet, so I was looking forward to a short hike to a gorgeous scenic overlook. Everything was going well until we reached the end of the easy trail and the path to the view was a steep downhill path over rocks and through trees. It was also getting dark, and I knew that if I needed one hand for a flashlight, that would only leave one hand for me to steady myself on this unfamiliar, steep trail. Not only that, I had a bad feeling about it. (And that's never a good thing...)

Chickie's Rock Park, home of the Alba twitch.

Stalked in the Woods

I watched as he walked out of sight down the trail. After a few minutes I realized it was very, very quiet, almost unnaturally so. It was also getting darker. There was no sign or sound of my friend from the trail. I really didn't want to stay where I was, but the prospect of walking back in the dark alone was less attractive than waiting there. Just as I was about to brave the walk back to the car, I heard my companion call out, "You missed a great view!"

We started our walk back and I swore I was hearing footsteps in the woods, off to our right. I began walking faster and my friend suddenly whispered, "Hey! Stop for a minute."

Quickly, I turned around and saw him looking to the right, peering into the dark woods. "Do you hear something?" he asked.

"I thought I heard footsteps," I replied.

My blood chilled when he looked right at me and said seriously, "So did I, but when we stopped, the footsteps stopped."

"Maybe it was our imagination," I said. "Let's just get back to the car." We picked up the pace. As we started walking faster, the footsteps started up again, this time to our left.

After a few minutes, he quietly told me to stop again. He was looking into the woods, trying to walk slowly while keeping an eye on the area the footsteps seemed to be coming from.

"What is it?" I asked.

"I don't know," he answered, "but we have to get out of here," he responded seriously, "whatever it is, I think it's tracking us."

That was all I needed to hear. We both ran back down the trail, out of the woods, and jumped into the car. After we had put a few miles between us and the trail, I asked him what he thought it was. It sounded more like a person than anything else, but he couldn't understand why a person would be tracking other people, and why people would not respond when we called out to them.

I knew nothing about the history, creepy or otherwise, of Chickie's Rock. All my companion knew was that it was supposed to be haunted. He wasn't sure of the background of the haunting or who it was supposed to be.

Research revealed some interesting things.

Historic Answers

The name Chickie's came from the Native American name for the area, "Chikiswalungo," or "the place of the crawfish."[8] Apparently, the Native Americans in the area viewed it as a haunted place and told stories of ghosts associated with the rock. The two main legends are of unfortunate lovers.

In one version, a young couple was not allowed to marry and chose to jump from the rocks to their deaths below, planning to reunite in eternity. Another less romantic legend tells of a Native maiden who fell in love with a white man. They would meet near the rock. One day, the man from her tribe that had been her suitor followed her. When he saw the two lovers, he became violently angry and murdered the man. The girl either jumped from the rock in despair or in an escape attempt, or she was thrown from the rock by her tribesman. The ghosts seen at the rock were of a couple.

Neither of these versions seemed like it would engender the type of predatory energy that seemed to watch us from the woods. I asked some other friends who had relatives in the Lancaster area. They all agreed that Chickie's was haunted, but they said it was haunted by victims of a trolley crash that happened there in the late 1800s. Although I agreed that it was possible for a tragedy like that to be the baseline for a haunting, it still didn't feel right. Whatever we experienced there was definitely more ominous than the lost souls from an accident.

It was years later when doing research for a project on Lancaster ghosts that I came across something that seemed like it may explain what we experienced that day. If I had known about these stories when I went down the trail at Chickie's Rock, there is no way I would have gone down there in the dark.

The Alba Twitch

Much of Pennsylvania was settled by German immigrants. Pennsylvania has retained some of this German heritage in place names like Heidelberg and East Berlin. It is visible in hex signs on the sides of barns and the dialect of German still spoken in small communities in Central Pennsylvania. Another sign of this heritage is werewolf legends. One legend is attached to the Hans Graf family plot near Marietta. It's said that old Hans was a werewolf and if you circle the graveyard seven times at midnight he will come out and chase you or eat you or something equally scary.

Some people claim the Alba Twitch is a form of a werewolf legend, which evolved as it was passed down, from the classic werewolf to the creature known as the Alba Twitch. Alba Twitches are said to be hominid beings about four feet tall. They are covered with hair, like a Bigfoot. The name comes from their fondness for apples, which they have been known to "snitch" from picnickers. My interpretation of the werewolf-Alba Twitch connection is the opposite of what I have heard. I think it is more logical that the German immigrants, familiar with the werewolf legends of Eastern Europe, encountered the Alba Twitch and figured it was the Pennsylvania version of the creature described in their folklore.

Are Alba Twitches real? The people who report experiences with them swear that they are and the only reported sightings I could find of these creatures in recent years were in the area of Chickie's Rock! In my opinion, the Alba Twitch, or Apple-Snitch as it is sometimes called, is a likely source for what we experienced.

Murder Swamp - New Castle

A swamp is a spooky place to begin with. Any step you take may land you up to your knees or higher in muddy water. There are strange sounds coming from the foliage. Paths seem to wind around and around and go nowhere. If you are unfamiliar with the area, it seems like you are passing the same places over and over again. Now imagine that not only do the natural features of the swamp threaten, but this swamp was once the dumping ground for a series of murders involving decapitation. The murderer was never caught and the victims dumped here were never identified. Their spirits are said to wander this swamp in search of something. Do they want justice? Do they search for their killer? No one has reported following one of the ghosts or interacting with them. Is it possible they are seeking to lead explorers towards undiscovered victims?

Headless Victims

The first victim was a young man, discovered on October 6, 1925. He was nude, headless, and had been there at least three weeks. His head was found two days later, but provided no help with identification. About ten days later, a headless male skeleton was found. Again, two days later, the missing skull was discovered with a female skull. The body of the female victim was never located.

Those unsolved murders, known locally as the headless murders, were a decade old when another headless male body was found at a railroad dump near New Castle Junction. The victim's head never turned up. The only clues in this case were some Pittsburgh and Cleveland newspapers found under the body, which were dated from July of 1933.

These Cleveland newspapers and the proximity to the railroad caused many to see a connection between these murders and a series in the Kingsbury Run area in Ohio, but the link was never formally made by investigators. They can't seem to agree on a connection or even which victims are related to the Kingsbury murders.

In October of 1939, another decapitated and decomposed male body surfaced in the Murder Swamp. There were some charred newspapers near the body; these were the September issues of a Youngstown, Ohio newspaper. The head of this victim was discovered in a nearby abandoned box car five days later. The nearby box car may provide a link with the Kingsbury case, but it may also be a deliberate attempt by the killer to mislead investigators into thinking the murder was connected with what was, by then, a famously unsolved case.

In November, one year later, another decapitated skeleton was found by a rabbit hunter in the swamp. The report of this new murder includes a reference to "eight other bodies found there in the last ten years."[9] The numbers only make sense if three other victims are included; these were three male decapitated victims found in boxcars in a nearby township in May of 1940. The article goes on to say that police believed that Cleveland, Ohio's Kingsbury Run killer "was responsible for some if not all of the New Castle slayings."[10]

There were some differences between this and the Kingsbury cases, foremost being that the Kingsbury murders generally occurred between 1934 and 1938 and all within one area, just as these new ones did. So the possibility of a copycat exists, especially with the sites that included railroad cars.

The first three swamp murders were likely connected with illegal alcohol and organized crime. In 1930, there was a similar case that was solved, in which a racketeer admitted to the murder of a man who had double crossed him. The man's body was found headless and his head was found two miles away.

I feel it is doubtful that all of these murders were committed by one person, as they span a period of fifteen years and vary widely in modus operandi. We will likely never know the identity of these victims, so we will probably never know who killed them. I think the answer lies somewhere in the Murder Swamp, waiting to be found.

Babes in the Woods - South Mountain

I remember being told this story by my grandmother, whose family was from the Carlisle area. She enjoyed telling stories about the Great Depression and how it affected people's lives. She loved telling us all about the Lindbergh baby and this story; the account of the man who was so desperate, he saw no way out of the Great Depression but murder and suicide.

My grandmother was a good storyteller, so it was easy for me to picture the scenes in my mind as they unfolded. The story started not in Pennsylvania, but in California, where an unemployed man with his girlfriend and three young daughters set out on a cross-country trip looking for any kind of work he could get. Their money and luck ran out in Pennsylvania. In the week before Thanksgiving Day, two men found three little girls lying under a blanket in the woods as if they had been put to bed.

The girls had been smothered and had not eaten for days before they died. No one knew who they were. No children had been reported missing by anyone in the area, so the town had a public viewing. People came from all over to see if they knew the little girls and also to pay their respects. It was in all the newspapers and on the radio. Every mother in the area hugged their own babies a little tighter.

A few days later they found the father and his girlfriend at a train station. They were also dead. The father had shot his girlfriend and then himself. They identified him and tied him to the three girls when they found the family's car and the one suitcase that contained the family's worldly belongings. The police traced the family back to California and the girls were identified as Norma, 12 years old, Dewilla, 10 years old, and 8-year-old Cordelia. Their father had killed the girls rather than watch them starve to death. He couldn't live with what he had done, so he killed his girlfriend to save her from being implicated and then himself.

The case was so touching that there was a sign put up by the roadside near where the little girls were found in the woods. They were given a funeral by the American Legion and the local Boy Scouts were pallbearers. The girls were buried in Westminster Cemetery with a big monument that is still there today.

I understand that some of the details that my grandmother related may be incorrect, but the story is true and she told it to me the way she remembered it. All accounts agree on the saddest part; that even today, when you go walking in the woods near that "Babes in the Woods" marker, you can hear the soft sobbing of what sounds like a little girl crying.

Creepy Country Inns

Whether you've come to stay the night, or just have a mind to have a bite to eat, the country inns of Pennsylvania may have the right atmosphere for you—but then again, you just might get a bit more than you bargained for... Regardless, the spirits of Pennsylvania welcome you.

Century Inn - Scenery Hill

This is the oldest inn along Route 40, otherwise known as the National Pike. It was built in 1794 and is one of the longest-operating taverns in the country. A family called Hill built it, so it was originally called Hill's Tavern.

When the inn was built, the road in front was an Indian trail. It took one day to travel twelve miles on the trail, so the towns were built twelve miles apart. If you drive west on Route 40 today and start at Brownsville, you will notice that it is twelve miles to Scenery Hill, and then twelve more to Washington. This was a popular overnight stop for stage coaches during the late 1700s and early 1800s. Some prominent Americans have stayed there, including presidents George Washington, Andrew Jackson, and James Polk.

The employees feel that the inn is haunted by the ghost of the previous owner. Her presence is the one that they feel most often, but here and there are other incidents that are not in character for her.

Century Inn in a spring snow shower.

Flying Artwork

For example, one night an entire wall of artwork flew off the wall and crashed to the floor in front of a bar full of patrons. All of the hooks were still in place and none of the glass was broken. One witness, who saw it, swore that everything came away from the wall at once, hovered in the air for a second and then fell to the floor. They were able to put everything back in its place and it has not happened since. It is not clear who or what may have caused this to happen, but it certainly seems like someone wanted attention.

The manager that we spoke with said that he sometimes feels the previous owner following him around as he goes about his duties. He even hears her footsteps. One day the feeling was so aggravating that he turned around and said, "Stop it! You're freaking me out!"

I asked him if this had any effect on the activity and he said that it stopped for that day, but has happened since. He described the previous owner as having had a great love for the inn and being very particular about how things were done. He thought she was following him to check up on things. He also speculated that it may be that she stays there because she is concerned about the future of the inn and wants it to continue as a family business.

The wonderful antique collection on display in rooms was put together by Mrs. Harrington, the previous owner. The current owner, also Mrs. Harrington, has added to the collection and maintains the business much as the first Mrs. Harrington did. The problem is that these businesses are largely a labor of love.

The artwork that crashed to the floor at the Century Inn.

Tucking In Guests

One of the other presences at the inn was experienced in the room above the bar area. Many times guests who had spent the night in that room would come down in the morning and compliment the employees on the excellent customer service there. They had all fallen asleep and kicked the blankets off and had woken to a little old lady who had come in to check on them and cover them up. Now, I would be very disturbed if I was sleeping in a hotel room and woke to someone over me pulling up my blankets, but no one who experienced this ever seemed bothered by it.

They maintain that this little old lady is not the previous owner. A psychic had visited the inn and told them that there was an old woman in the upstairs room who was waiting for her son to return from the Civil War. The psychic was able to communicate with the old woman and told her that her son had been killed in the war and had already crossed over into the spirit world. She encouraged the woman to cross over as well and it appears that she did. They have received no reports of the little old lady checking on guests since the psychic was there.

A Hearth With a Focus

The one room where I felt a presence in the Century Inn was the old kitchen. It is currently used as a dining room and contains a large eighteenth-century fireplace with all the tools needed for preparing meals in the 1700s. When the Harringtons first purchased the inn, the fireplace was behind a wall. During the renovations they opened the wall and uncovered a time capsule. Someone had walled up the fireplace with all of the tools inside. It appears today much as it did when it was discovered. Perhaps when the fireplace and the tools were uncovered, a dormant spirit was awakened. Also, it is odd that the entire fireplace and its contents were walled up. Was there a reason this was done? Was this hearth a focus for paranormal activity in the past?

One theory about ghosts and haunting holds that somehow emotional events are able to imprint themselves on the walls and fixtures of a building. If this theory is valid, consider the amount of emotional and other energy that would have been released when this hearth, which would have been the center of activity in the eighteenth century, was uncovered.

Another legend associated with the Century Inn is that when it snows, unexplained footprints can be seen leading away from the inn. My second visit to the inn was during a snowstorm. I did not see any footprints leading away from the inn, but my attention was drawn to an old well at the side.

A Coin in a Well

Many old homes that I have investigated, including the one I grew up in, had paranormal activity centered around old wells. I am unsure why this is, but wells are a powerful symbol of life and rebirth, so maybe the energy that surrounds wells is conducive to spirits. It may even be that they serve as portals between this world and the next. Wells have been used for scrying and healing as well as wish-granting throughout history. Wishes are granted by the spirit of the well, who is paid by tossing a coin into the water. I remembered hearing an old wives' tale as a child about wells. Failing to cover a well properly, or looking back at it after getting water from it, or leaning over the side to look in can cause the spirit of the well to come after you. The well, as you can see, was partially uncovered. I reached into my pocket for a coin and tossed one into the opening, just in case. I didn't want the spirit of the well following me home.

Century Inn
2715 East National Pike
Scenery Hill, PA 15360
724-945-5180
www.centuryinn.com

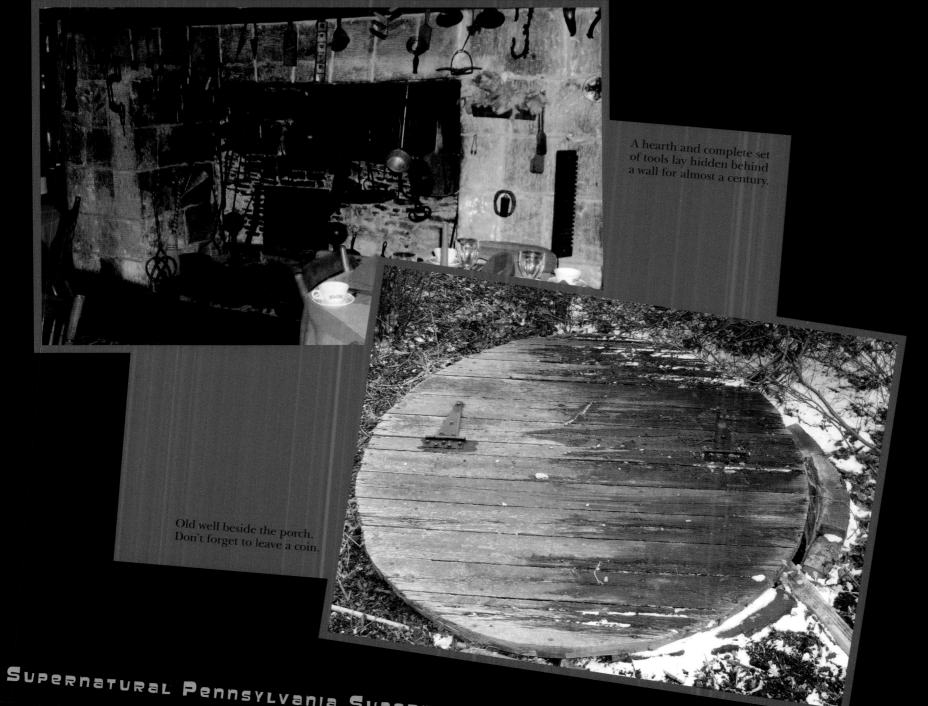

A hearth and complete set of tools lay hidden behind a wall for almost a century.

Old well beside the porch. Don't forget to leave a coin.

General Warren Inn - Malvern

The first thing I want to say about the General Warren Inn is that it is, in my opinion, very haunted. The next thing I want to say is that the General Warren Inn is not, and never was, the General Wayne Inn. The General Wayne Inn is in Merion, Pennsylvania, and is now a synagogue. The whole story of the haunting there can be read in my book, *Philly's Main Line Haunts*.

The General Warren Inn is in Malvern, Pennsylvania, at the other end of Philadelphia's Main Line. It was built in 1745 to serve the traffic on the Old Lancaster Pike. It was originally called the Admiral Vernon, after a British Naval Officer and was renamed the Admiral Warren after a hero of the French and Indian War. As the colonists began to polarize in the time before the American Revolution broke out, the Admiral Warren Inn became a Tory, or Loyalist gathering place. Later, in an attempt to appease the Whigs, it was renamed the General Warren Inn in honor of a Patriot hero.

The Inn was a popular stop on the old turnpike until the railroads made travel by coach obsolete. The Inn continued to operate as a tavern and inn off and on over the years, and it remains today as one of the finest places to dine and stay in the area. It is also one of the most haunted.

We had the opportunity to stay overnight – alone – in the General Warren Inn, and we took it. We would be the first formal investigators there, and hoped that we would have something to share with the owner the next morning. It was a big place and there were only two of us, my co-founder Mary Gasparo and I, so we had our work cut out for us. Before we left for dinner we went through the whole inn, turning out all of the lights and making sure all the doors and drawers were closed.

Welcome to the haunted General Warren Inn.

Lights Out... Lights On

When we returned, we began going through all of the rooms on the first and then the second floor. On the second floor we noticed that the light over the sink in the middle suite was on. There was no way this could have been on when we left, as we could see it from the stairs. We walked down the hall to the Presidential Suite and saw that the two drawers in the TV stand were now open and the desk light was on. On the third floor, one of the bathroom lights was on. Not anything big, but just enough to make us doubt whether we had checked every light, drawer, and door, even though we knew we had. We again closed the drawers, shut off the lights, and prepared to begin the vigil.

A light was inexplicably turned on in one of the baths.

The threshold of the bedroom where I got slimed.

Third-Floor Haunts and Second Floor Motion

We decided to begin on the third floor and work our way back down. It is rumored that just prior to the Battle of Paoli, some British soldiers had captured the local blacksmith, brought him to the Inn, and tortured him in the attic, which is now the third floor, to get the location of General Wayne's encampment. The blacksmith's ghost is said to haunt the third floor rooms.

Things were pretty quiet until we got to the Franklin Suite. As soon as we entered, I was uncomfortable. Mary was talking about where to sit and do an EVP session and I was frozen in the doorway between the sitting room and the bedroom.

"What's wrong?" she asked. "You have that *deer in the headlights* look."

"I don't like this. I feel like something is right behind me. If we sit in there I will have to have my back to the room."

"Okay," she said, "Let's sit in the sitting room then."

We took one step and then we both froze and looked at each other.

"Did you hear that?" we both asked at the same time. We had heard what sounded like a low growl. Now I was really uncomfortable, but decided to just go ahead and do the EVP session. Maybe things were about to get really active.

As I stepped over the threshold into the bedroom I became aware of a slimy, clear substance all over my right hand and my digital recorder. I asked Mary if she saw it and she pointed out that it was also on my shirt. Almost as soon as we looked at it, it evaporated. I do not know what it was and I have never had that happen to me before. It wasn't on anything else in the room and now it was gone. I decided to take a break and get myself grounded; this had really shaken me up for some reason.

We had left a motion-sensitive camera in the second-floor hallway while we investigated the third floor. When we returned to the room where we were staying, we checked it and found that it had gone off. The photo was completely white as if something had obscured the entire front of the camera.

Margaret and the British Soldier

We decided to make our next stop the bar area, where we planned to hold a ghost box session. A ghost box is a radio that has been modified to continuously scan the dial, providing a ready source of audio snippets for spirits to turn into audible communication. We asked if there were British soldiers there, and the response was a very clear, "One."

We also received communication from a woman named Margaret who said she fell down. This was significant because another one of the legends associated with the inn is that of a woman named Margaret who is said to have fallen down the stairs and died in the mid-nineteenth century.

The remaining few hours of the night were uneventful, but after the earlier excitement I think we were glad to get some rest. Although we did not determine whether the legend of the blacksmith was true, we did encounter some intriguing insight into the spirits that were there; the British soldier, Margaret, and whoever slimed me upstairs.

I did some checking into what that could possibly have been, and one interesting idea was that it was ectoplasm. When I use this term, I am referring to the substance believed to be created when a ghost comes in contact with the physical world. It is described as a slimy, syrupy substance that is created when a spirit passes through matter. Did a spirit pass through my digital recorder? The recorder and my hand were covered with it. But upon listening to the recorder later, there were no EVPs from that particular time.

The spirits here are a fascinating group and I look forward to getting to know them better.

General Warren Inn
16 Village Way
Malvern, PA 19355
610-296-3637
www.generalwarren.com

Is this the fatal staircase?

Stottsville Inn - Pomeroy

This picturesque Victorian Inn and restaurant seems like an ideal setting for a good ghost story. It looks like it should have a weeping woman in white or maybe a brooding man in black.

The Stottsville Inn was originally built in the early 1740s by Thomas Truman. It was rebuilt in 1858, by David Stott, given the Victorian look and the name, the Stottsville Hotel. When Mr. Stott retired, his sons took over the hotel business and the inn enjoyed a great reputation and was visited by two U.S. Presidents, Grover Cleveland and Benjamin Harrison.

According to the Inn's website, "on Wednesday, December 17, 1890, Josephine Stott Chandler married Horace G. Emery in a ceremony held at the inn. Noted in the Inn's ledgers as "A day which will be remembered…," the place must have been an extra special setting for a wedding ceremony."[11] This is where the legend starts.

Strange suicide note or not-so-funny joke?

Josephine and Horace

According to tradition, Josephine was a beautiful young woman who was unfaithful to her husband, Horace. He caught her and murdered her in her room and then killed himself, leaving what has to be one of the strangest suicide notes in history:

The text of the note reads:

I love, love, love you. You are the dream of my life. Come with me to the shoe store and I will make love to you.
Love, Horace.

Then there is an extremely odd post script;

P.S., I can't live without you so I will commit suicide in the barn. I will bite a cow's leg and he will kick me in the head and kill me. For without you, life is nothing.

I have not been able to track down the origin of this sordid tale. Research into the history of the inn and the lives of Josephine and Horace reveal facts that indicate this fanciful tale of adultery, murder, and suicide were just that – someone's fancy.

Josephine was really the daughter of Maris Taylor and Elizabeth Stott and they did own the Stottsville Inn according to 1870 census records. The Chester County Historical Society records have copies of Josephine and Horace's wedding announcement. They were married on December 18, 1890, at the home of the bride. The next mention of Josephine is in 1893, when it was reported that she had died "after several weeks of suffering"[12] at her sisters' home. The Chester County Death records have this entry; "Emery, Josephine C., white, female, 37, married, West Chester, 1893/07/06, Coatesville, Bronchitis".[13]

At that point I was thinking, "Well, the murder part is made up, but maybe he did commit suicide after she died so tragically just three years after their wedding." Further research revealed that the suicide part of the story was not true either. The census records of 1900 show that Horace Emery was alive and well and living with his mother in Coatesville.

So who haunts the Stottsville Inn? It is possible that Josephine and Horace remain there, trying to clear their names of these accusations of adultery, murder, and suicide.

The current owner, Jack Selah, and the employees of the Inn are quick to tell you that the legend has no basis in fact whatsoever. Josephine was not murdered and Horace did not commit suicide. Mr. Selah is a very friendly and open gentleman who gladly gave me a tour of the entire building. He stays in the inn, so he began telling me that in the room he normally stays in, he often wakes up in the morning to find that his personal items have been moved around. Guests who have stayed overnight in the room have reported similar incidents. He is unsure who it is that may be haunting the inn.

An Attic Haunt

I felt strongly that we should have a look in the attic. As we ascended the narrow stairs to the upper floor, he informed me that the attic has been the site of the most significant unexplained activity. He said that chairs placed in one area have slid across the floor to another part of the attic. As we entered the room, I was met with a strong feeling that whoever was up there liked their privacy and felt that we were intruding. They liked to have things their way and did not appreciate having others walk in unannounced. The owner admitted that he also felt as if someone were staring at us and wondering why we came in there. He said that they don't normally go into the attic and everyone who has spent any time up there has reported a very uncomfortable feeling.

It was obvious that the owner was very uncomfortable up there. I tried to reassure him by telling whoever was with us that we were just there to look around. We were not there to stay or to change anything; we just wanted to look around and take some photos. I tried to get a clearer picture of the spirit that inhabits the attic as I took some photos. The feeling was that it was a male spirit, which was at odds with the picture I was getting of the attic having once been where the female servants slept.

The feeling of being an intruder began to get stronger and I was beginning to think that maybe he had hidden something up there that he was trying to protect. I tried to reassure him that I just wanted to tell his story and take some photos. When I listened to my recording later, I got a chill as I heard a male voice respond to my statement that I wanted to tell his story. The voice was gruff and harsh, "Did you?" Now I was really wondering who this man was. Was he upset about the tall tales that had been published in the past about the ghosts at the Stottsville Inn? As we descended the stairs from the attic, I saw a shadowy form dash down the stairs in front of us. I mentioned this to Mr. Selah, who nodded as if this was something that was not uncommon.

Someone in the attic wanted to be left alone.

A strong presence emanated from this room.

A Second-Floor Room

Another area of interest to me was a guest room at the top of the stairs on the second floor. As I approached this room I felt pressure on my throat, which grew stronger as I tried to enter the room. The owner said that no one else has reported feeling that, but a local group of paranormal investigators that have researched the activity there did get some anomalous photos in that room. That is one area that I felt needed more exploration. That would have to wait for another day, however, as I was anxious to see the downstairs areas as well.

The Bar

I asked the owner if there was any paranormal activity downstairs. He replied that he often felt as if someone were following him when he entered the bar or the dining room when he was alone in the building. He also said that one night a group of girls were having a get together in the bar and had taken several photos. When they later reviewed the photos, they contacted the inn because in one of their group photos they saw a white circular form that was in such a position that it seemed to be another face alongside theirs. He asked the hostess to show me the photo and it did clearly show a white circular form. I wasn't lucky enough to have anything show up in my photos of the area, but I did have the whisper of a male voice on my recording say, "Hi!" after I placed my things onto the table in the bar.

In further support of the bar area being a focus for activity, another unexplained voice was on my audio recording from that day. It was recorded while I was waiting for the hostess/bartender to get a drink for the only customer sitting at the bar that day. While she was occupied, he turned to me and asked, "So, is it haunted?" I responded that there were a couple of areas in the building that I felt required further exploration. Between his question and my response was a quick female whisper, "Goodbye for now."

The Dining Room

The hostess told me that she had also sensed a presence in the dining room. Every time she went in there she felt as if she was intruding. One day she got tired of feeling watched and told whoever it was to just go away. She said she hasn't felt the presence since then. They have a cleaning woman on Mondays who often brings her son to the inn with her. He plays in the empty rooms of the inn while she does the weekly heavy cleaning. One day her son came running over to her to tell her there was someone in the dining room who was scaring him. Concerned that someone had entered the inn, she quickly ran over to the dining room and found it completely empty. A check of the inn and the doors found the doors still locked and the structure completely empty except for them. The little boy has since refused to go into the dining room.

I left the inn that day still unsure of who the resident spirits were. The feeling in the inn is that they are people who lived and worked there and are still going about the business of their daily lives though long dead. Perhaps a more directed and lengthy attempt at communication with the spirits I encountered that day would give us more clues to their identity and their purpose.

Stottsville Inn
3512 Strasburg Road
Coatesville, PA 19320
610-857-4090
www.stottsville.com

The seemingly empty dining room.

Hamanassett Bed and Breakfast Inn - Chester Heights

The name *Hamanassett* comes from the first resident, Dr. Charles Meigs. He built this home in what was then the country when he retired from practicing medicine in 1861. "It was named after a river in Connecticut where his ancestors had settled."[14]

From the beginning this estate was known for its beauty and hospitality and the current owners, Glenn and Ashley Mon, have upheld this tradition there.

We were fortunate to have been given the opportunity to investigate this place and we quickly saw why it would be difficult for anyone to want to leave. We started on the second floor and right away noticed a presence at the end of the hallway, right near a swinging door marked private.

View of the hallway where we felt a presence at the Hamanassett.

The Windsor Room

The other area of interest on this floor was the Windsor Room. In this room I picked up on the presence of a woman named Mary, who said that this was her room and she was staying there. As we walked toward a short hallway that led to the bathroom, we all became very uncomfortable as if we were entering an area that was private. We captured two EVPs from this area that indicated that the spirit of the woman there wanted her privacy. She told us, very politely, to get out.

The energy near the bathroom felt very confusing, as if this had been two parts of the house or used to be two separate rooms but was now one. (Later, when we were shown some old floor plans, we saw that it had been two separate rooms at one time.) While we were in that room we all heard the distinct sound of the metal door knob turning. There was no one else on the floor. Was it someone else trying to make their presence known?

In addition, I found that Dr. Meigs' wife was named Mary. A check of the census reports seemed to indicate that she was the only Mary that lived there. Perhaps this had been her room at one time.

My daughter Aarika, who has trained with us as a psychic investigator, was with us and she began picking up on something else about the woman named Mary. She saw her with two little boys. Aarika felt that one of them had passed away and that the lady was sad because of that. She saw the two little boys as the same age. In doing research about this, we found an interesting parallel with this while doing research into the Meigs family.

The Meigs' had ten children all together. In 1819, they had a little boy that they named William Montgomery. He passed away in March of 1824, when he was four years old. In April of 1826, they had another son and named him William Montgomery. He survived to adulthood. We believe Aarika was picking up on something from Mary's life that had affected her deeply – the death of a little boy so loved that they named another son after him.

Aarika and Laurie take some readings in the Windsor Room.
Photo courtesy of Mary Gasparo.

The Tudor Room

When we moved to the third floor, we quickly determined that The Tudor Room was the center of a lot of activity. Mary, one of our psychic members, saw the image of a man with a beard on the far wall at the same time as I picked up on a violent confrontation that had happened between a man and a woman there. The images were so strong that I had to leave the room to collect myself. We attempted to communicate with the spirits in that room. I felt that his name was Charles. Although I know that Dr. Meigs' name was Charles, I did not feel it was him that was the source of the image that I received.

Further research into the history revealed two other men named Charles who were associated with the house. In the latter part of the nineteenth century, the estate was purchased by the Dohan family, who lived there for the next 130 years. The first Charles was Charles Barton Keen, the architect who carried out the renovations at the house in the early part of the twentieth century. The second Charles was another doctor, Dr. Charles Dohan, who was born about 1868. He never married and his residence is recorded as being at Hamanassett, with his mother, until his death in 1920. During his life he was a practicing allopath, "a broad category of medical practice that is sometimes called Western medicine, biomedicine, scientific medicine, or modern medicine"[15], and he was also the leader of the Lima Hunt Club, which was headquartered at Hamanassett.

Although tradition has it that it is likely Dr. Meigs that haunts the place, because he is known to have said he hated to leave it, I feel it is equally possible that the Charles we encountered was Dr. Charles Dohan.

The wall of the Tudor Room where Mary saw a man's face.

An Open Door Policy?

When we returned to the second floor, we saw that the swinging door marked private was now standing open. Everyone had gone upstairs together and we had a video of the area before we went up that showed the door closed.

Did the spirit Mary open the door or was it another spirit? I had picked up on a presence near that door earlier. Later, when we spoke with the owners, they indicated that this was the door to their private quarters. They reported experiencing a good deal of unexplainable and unusual events there.

The Hamanassett Bed and Breakfast is excellently run and most assuredly still plays host to at least one past resident. This inn would make an excellent base for exploring the very haunted Brandywine Valley.

**Hamanassett Bed and Breakfast
and Carriage House**
115 Indian Springs Drive
Media, PA 19063
877-836-8212
www.hamanassett.com

When we returned from investigating the Tudor Room, the hall door was open.

Spooky Haunted Historic Sites

It's time to take a look back into Pennsylvania's historic past to see where some of the hauntings have begun. For as you know, those who do not understand the past are doomed to repeat it in the future. Could that be happening in Pennsylvania as we speak?

A shuttered Cliveden, as it appeared during the battle.

Cliveden - Germantown, Philadelphia

This gorgeous example of Georgian architecture was once the scene of a fierce battle. The house was owned by Benjamin Chew, a figure whose allegiance was questionable. It is known that he was not a supporter of the Revolution. According to University of Pennsylvania records, "In 1754 Chew moved to Philadelphia and again established a thriving law practice. During this period, Chew represented the interests of the Penn family, and like them, left his Quaker faith to join the Church of England."[16] It is likely that he did this to try and protect his sizeable assets. Many people in the colonies considered themselves to be British citizens and remained loyal to England during the Revolutionary War.

In 1777, the British were on their way to taking Philadelphia after their victory at Brandywine and the Patriots were trying hard to hold on to the city. When a detachment of British troops realized Patriots were about to attack, they decided to use the Chew house as cover and they holed up inside to fire at Washington and his troops. At the time, Chew was under arrest in New Jersey on suspicion of treason. In spite of fierce efforts on the part of the Patriots to capture the Chew house, they were unsuccessful. After several hours of charges, battering rams and musket fire, approximately 56 Patriots were dead and British reinforcements had arrived to chase away the remainder of Washington's men.

In 1779, Chew sold his mansion and then repurchased it in 1797. I suspect that he sold it to avoid it being seized by the Americans. His repurchase of the property after the suspicions about his allegiance died down add support to this theory. His resumption of ownership was the beginning of a Chew family ownership that carried on unbroken until 1972, when it was donated to the National Trust. The house has undergone renovations and restoration over the years, but reminders of that long-ago battle are not hard to find.

A Portrait in Blood

The imposing entry way still bears the mark of that battle as holes from musket fire are visible to the right as you enter. In an upstairs bedroom there is the blood of a dying British soldier. These marks are said to be a portrait of the dying man's wife. He drew it in his blood as he was dying there, so that the last thing he would see was his loved one's face.

Are these the only things left from that battle? Some say no. Over the years people who have lived and worked at Cliveden have reported seeing ghostly British soldiers, still defending their position in the Chew mansion. Are these soldiers the only reminders of Cliveden's past?

A Severed Mystery

One rather gruesome ghost legend said to stem from the battle is that of the headless woman. The story goes that an old woman, who had seen the approaching armies and feared the worst, decided to hide in the basement of Cliveden rather than chance trying to get by the troops without being seen. When the British soldiers entered the basement, they found her and one of them, berserk with battle rage, beheaded her and ran from the house, carrying her severed head and screaming, shaking the head at the Patriots in an effort to frighten them off. Interesting as this story is, an examination of documents turned up no reports of sightings of this ghost. The origin of this legend remains a mystery, and it is doubtful that it has any basis in truth.

Anne Sofia Penn Chew

Although the headless woman has not been seen, another woman has made her presence known at Cliveden. This female spirit is said to be Anne Sofia Penn Chew, the granddaughter of the first Benjamin Chew. She worked hard to preserve Cliveden. This was no easy task. When her father died, the estate was contested. Her brother, "Bad Ben" removed and sold many of the most important family heirlooms and she, with her nephew, managed to locate the items and purchase them back. Some say she is still watching over her beloved heirloom, Cliveden. She makes her presence known on the main staircase and in the large bedroom suite on the second floor of the mansion.

Very often the people who work at Cliveden have found the doors to her former bedroom closed, even though they are always left open. I felt that she did this to protect her privacy.

As I stood in her former bedroom listening to Mr. Fink, the education director, tell me about Anne Chew, I noticed that we were now surrounded by a cloud of light, floral fragrance. He said that he has been told that Anne has been associated with the unexplained smell of perfume. I was pleased that she chose to welcome me to her home by listening to our conversation.

During the tour, I also became aware of a lady on the front stairs. Was this Anne Chew? Mr. Fink confirmed that some people have reported seeing a lady there that resembles the portrait of Anne. Does she still stand at the top of the stairs to receive visitors? This photo would seem to indicate that she might.

I felt the need to go into the room towards the front of the house. When I asked Mr. Fink what was in there, he told me that there was normally a bed in that room and then added that it was the room with the portrait in blood. We walked over to the wall and he pointed out the area, which is covered with Plexiglas. At first, the portrait is difficult to pick out, but once the features are identified, the face of a woman in profile is clear. Cliveden has had the material tested and the lab report confirmed that the portrait was painted in blood from a living entity, although it was not specific as to whether it was human or not. In addition, the lab was able to date the blood as being from the late eighteenth century.

Locked Out

We then walked to the first floor and Mr. Fink pointed out some of the bullet holes in the walls of the main hall. He tried to open the door of an adjoining room but was not able to. While we were trying to make the old key work in the lock I felt like someone was watching our efforts and was very amused by them. When I reviewed the recording later, I noticed that right when we gave up a voice whispered, "Oh, my gosh!" It sounded like they were impatient with us and couldn't understand why we were unable to work the lock.

There was one other area of interest that I wanted to ask about. On a previous tour, I had felt as if there was a presence in the back hallway by the servant's stairs. When I asked him about the area, he informed me that this was the only door the Patriots were able to penetrate. They were killed and the area was fortified, but it was the scene of some fierce and bloody fighting.

The basement of Cliveden is dark and maze-like, with rooms that lead off of each other and seem to be haphazardly arranged. One section of the basement in particular radiated that energy that I have learned to associate with a spirit presence.

The staircase where the ghost of a woman has been seen.

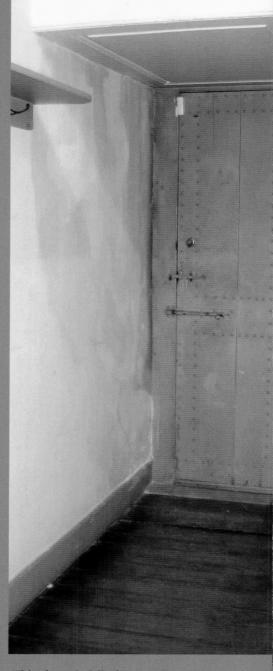

This alcove is full of energy from the fighting and death there.

Nearly every wall bears the marks of that long ago battle.

Friendly Fire or Something Else?

Mr. Fink patiently stood while I tried to get some more specifics. The picture that I was receiving was of a British soldier who had been dragged to that room, dying. The message I received from him was clear. He had been shot by his fellow soldiers. Mr. Fink allowed that there was likely a lot of confusion during the battle and it was possible some shootings by friendly fire had occurred. That was really not the feeling I had, but it was fleeting and I let it go for another day.

The next time I visited Cliveden they had the third floor open for visitors. It was interesting, but not haunted. The stairs and the door that had been breached were still giving off that air of some unseen resident or soldier lurking, but the third floor seemed very light and airy, despite the numerous bullet holes that remained in the window wells.

It was after we returned to the ground floor that I gained some possible insight into our friend in the basement. I remarked that I still felt that the haunted spots in the house were the side door by the servant's stairs and the basement. Mr. Fink commented that other paranormal investigators had reached similar conclusions. As we walked around admiring the woodwork and the newly restored areas of the house, the meaning behind the vision I had in the basement finally came to me. Maybe it was because our visit almost coincided with the date of the Battle of Germantown.

"How did the Patriots know that the British were hiding in here?" I asked.

Mr. Fink turned to me and answered, "That is a good question. During the re-enactment we have a couple British soldiers in red coats lounging on the lawn. When the Americans come into view, they run inside."

A simple explanation, but I know that both armies of the American Revolution had extensive intelligence-gathering networks. It is not easy for me to accept that the British had no idea the Patriot forces were advancing right up Germantown Avenue. It is even more difficult to believe that the Americans took them by surprise, lounging on the lawn right outside their main stronghold.

Is it possible that the soldier who I saw shot in the basement was part of that intelligence network and he was found out by his fellow soldiers or even his commander? As I asked the question, I already knew the answer. Someone had found out and he had been held in the basement, under questioning, when the battle started in earnest. Was he shot accidentally in the melee or accidentally-on-purpose by someone who felt he had now outlived his usefulness as an informer since the Americans were right outside?

Every time I visit this gorgeous Georgian mansion, I find out that those in charge there have uncovered more of its history. As the story unfolds and more paranormal research is conducted there, maybe the whole story from my visions will be made clear.

Cliveden
6401 Germantown Avenue
Philadelphia, PA 19144
(215) 848-1777
http://cliveden1767.wordpress.com

Rock Ford Plantation - Lancaster

This remarkably well-preserved mansion is located in a park near the Conestoga River. I visited Rock Ford with my friend and associate, Dinah Roseberry. Neither of us had ever been to the plantation before and when we first saw it, we both paused and stared for a moment, taking in the beauty of the architecture and its seemingly natural place in the landscape.

Tea For George

We were greeted by Mr. Sam Slaymaker and shown into the main hall. My first thought upon entering was, "George Washington was here!" It was something the spirits in the house were very proud of. It was clear that there was the presence of a woman with us and she seemed very sad, but wanted us to know that the Father of our country had been there.

I had to ask Mr. Slaymaker about George Washington, and he indicated that it is believed that he may have been there. The house was built by Edward hand, who had been the Adjutant General to George Washington during the last year of the American Revolution. After the war, he became active in Lancaster politics and from 1785 to 1794 he built and expanded what is now known as Rock Ford plantation.

To further answer my question about whether George Washington had ever been there, Mr. Slaymaker said that it was recorded that in 1791, while the house was still under construction, George came to visit the Hands and had tea with them. The exact location of this meeting was not recorded, but they like to think it may have happened there at the house. I offered that even if the house had not been completed, surely Edward Hand would have taken his friend George over to show him the progress being made on his magnificent new home and the extent of his property holdings.

Whatever the record reflects so far, let my record reflect that when I visited Rock Ford, I was told by an elegant and sad lady that haunts the place that George Washington had been there.

Sadly, that may have been one of the few happy occasions at the plantation. Edward Hand died from a sudden and severe illness in 1802, only eight years after completion of his grand home. His wife was left with the children and no way to support herself, other than the plantation farm.

General Hand's country estate, Rock Ford.

Stain on the floor that was found to be boot black.
Photo courtesy of Dinah Roseberry.

Suicide

The reason Rock Ford was so incredibly well-preserved was because of its reputation for being haunted. The reputation stemmed from a suicide. For many years it had been assumed that the suicide occurred in an upstairs room because of some stains on the floor that were believed to be blood.

Recently they took some scrapings from the stains to be analyzed by a lab. The analysis showed that the stains were not blood; they were boot black. It is not clear when the stains became associated with the suicide, but it is likely that they were there when it was sold out of the family in 1810. Since it was known that the death had occurred in the house, it was assumed that the stains were blood. The victim of suicide was John Hand, who is said to have taken his own life with a gun when he was about 25 years old.

As we stood in the room with the stain, discussing the stain and the suicide, Dinah's K-2 meter began to flash. This indicated a sudden change in the electromagnetic field around us. These spikes in electromagnetic energy are normally associated with paranormal activity or the presence of a ghost.

I felt as if someone was trying to get our attention. As I concentrated, I became aware of the presence of a young man who appeared in shadow. He did not want to reveal his face. He was standing in the hallway, pointing towards the stairs as if he wanted us to go down. I asked Mr. Slaymaker if they had ever discovered where the suicide had really occurred, and he indicated that they had concluded that the suicide probably occurred in the downstairs parlor rather than upstairs.

As we discussed the incident, the shadowy man in the hallway became more agitated and began to pace up and down. "No, no!" was what I was getting as he walked back and forth, shaking his head. I tried to discern more details, but he did not want to reveal much. The general impression I was left with was that his death may not have been a suicide at all. He did show me brief images from his life, which included a great deal of drinking and gambling. Did he commit suicide in despair over a gambling loss or did he die accidentally or at the hands of some unknown other? The only thing that I was certain of when we left his presence was that there was much, much more to that story.

Playtime

The shadowy form of John Hand was not the only ghost that roamed the halls of Rock Ford. Residents and caretakers have also reported seeing and hearing ghostly children playing in what was once the playroom. There is an old puzzle on the floor that has been known to be inexplicably put together when it is left apart.

Katherine Hand died in 1791 at age 12. Although she died in Lancaster, it was not clear whether they were living at Rock Ford at the time or not. Margaret Hand died in 1800 at age 11 at Rock Ford. Are they the children that the caretaker's children reported playing with? Are their hands the ones that place the puzzle pieces in their places? They must have been playing hide and seek with us that day, because they did not make their presence known while we were upstairs.

The puzzle in the children's room is sometimes inexplicably put together.

The Old Kitchen

Our visit to Rock Ford ended in the old kitchen in the basement. As Mr. Slaymaker pointed out various features of the hearth and explained how the kitchen would have functioned in the early 1800s, we stood talking. Suddenly, we all heard a distinct shuffling sound from outside the door. We stopped and went to look, but there was nothing there. We went back to resume the tour and there it was again. This time we made a more thorough investigation of the area, but we could not find any possible source for the shuffling sound.

Mr. Slaymaker said there was no tradition of ghostly activity there, but there is no denying what we heard. The shuffling sound was reminiscent of an old straw broom dragging across the floor. Were we hearing an echo of a long-ago event or was some spectral kitchen maid continuing to go about her duties all these years later?

In spite of the sad stories, Rock Ford doesn't have a depressing atmosphere. The spirits that linger there seem to just continue on with their lives and want to share their stories. If you visit Rock Ford, make sure to keep an open mind and ear for them.

Historic Rock Ford Plantation
881 Rock Ford Road
Lancaster, PA 17602
717-392-7223
www.rockfordplantation.org

The Indian Rock

As we were leaving, Mr. Slaymaker asked us if we knew about the Native American burial ground up the hill from the plantation. We hadn't. He didn't know too much about it, other than some park workers had been putting in a water line and discovered human remains. The remains were examined and found to be Native American. They were reburied after the work was done.

We weren't sure where the burial ground was, just that it was up the hill. He also described a large rock memorial with a plaque telling about it. After a few wrong turns and a consultation with some passing park workers, we found it.

It was at the highest point there, overlooking the river on one side and the countryside on the other. As we stepped towards the rock, there was a definite feeling of entering a sacred space.

The plaque reads:

This high point of land overlooking the Conestoga River and Mill Creek was used by certain American Indians as a cemetery during the first quarter of the 18th century. The accidental discovery of this important archaeological and historical site was made in 1979 by county park construction workers while laying a water line. Archaeologists were called in and their careful excavation revealed that at least twelve Indian men, women, and children were buried here.

We walked around the area, trying to see if any vibrations from that burial ground could be felt. All we felt was a quiet peacefulness that made us want to speak in a whisper. We didn't see anything, but there was a strong sense of being watched. Was it one of those Native American spirits watching to guard against further intrusion? Just in case, I sent out a peaceful message to whoever was there that we were just paying our respects, nothing more.

The stone memorializing the Native Americans buried there.

Nemacolin Castle - Brownsville

I remember the first time I saw Nemacolin Castle. We were driving east on Route 40, on our way to Ohiopyle Park. As we crossed the bridge over the Monongahela River, I saw a castle there on the opposite side, emerging from the mist.

For a minute I thought it was my imagination, so I asked my father, "What's that place?"

He said, "Let's go find out!" (This is one of the many reasons I still love spending time with my Dad. He is always ready for an adventure.)

The castle is gorgeous from the outside. I couldn't wait to get inside and look around. And what castle doesn't have a ghost or two roaming around? It looked like we were the only people there that day, but there was a sign saying they were open for tours. I could hardly keep myself from running over to the door. The tour guide that met us was an encyclopedia of information about the castle and the whole area. This was going to be good.

The castle was built in 1789, but was not the first structure on that site. It was constructed on the site of a Native American mound, one of several in the area. The Monongahela Valley is considered part of the larger Ohio Valley complex of Indian Mounds. The town of Brownsville, where Nemacolin Castle is, was originally called Red Fort.

It is not clear from historical records exactly what the fort was, but consensus is that it was most likely a fortified Native village. The property now occupied by the castle is believed to be the actual site of the village; it is referred to as the residence of Nemacolin, a the Native American who helped white settlers set the course for what is now Route 40. There were other mound sites within easy distance from it. Additionally, the journal of a local settler, Joshua Gilpin mentions "Native American burial remains unearthed in the construction of cellars in the vicinity of Nemacolin Castle"[17].

Like many homes of this era, the castle was built in stages. What is currently the sitting room fireplace is thought to predate the castle and is believed to be part of the Fort Byrd structure that occupied this spot until the castle was begun by Jacob Bowman in 1789.

Nemacolin Castle still surrounded by a stone wall.

Jacob commissioned the building of a three-story house and he lived there until his death in 1847. The Bowmans owned slaves, like several other families in the area. Rumors of Underground Railroad activity have been heard, but there is no documentation to back this up. There are several "secret" rooms in the castle, but this in itself does not indicate they were used for the Underground Railroad. Many old homes that were built in stages, as the castle was, contain unusual features, like bricked up windows in stairwells and closets behind fireplaces.

Jacob's youngest son, Nelson inherited the house. Nelson got married late in life to Elizabeth Dunn and they added the Victorian wing, including the towers, to make it the castle we see today. He had inherited a great deal of money from his father. Elizabeth died in the house in 1889 and was buried in the nearby Christ Church cemetery.

Tiffany Pride

In the back of the house is a beautiful parlor with a Tiffany lamp and a table set as if for tea. The spirit of a woman was in this area when we were there. She seemed to be very proud of the lamp and the mantle on the fireplace. This room was her favorite room in the house. Could this have been the spirit of Elizabeth?

Nelson left the castle to his son Charles and his wife, Lelia, who have been compared to The Great Gatsby because of the lifestyle of partying and traveling they led. Charles Bowman lived there until 1945, when he died after being injured in a fall in Pittsburgh. He was brought back to Brownsville General Hospital, but he never made it back home."[18]

So, three generations of Bowmans lived in the house until 1959, when Mrs. Lelia Bowman died. The castle was made into a museum according to her wishes.

The Ghosts

Ghost stories were not part of the regular tour, but there were several areas where I felt a presence.

The Storage Area

The storage area was one place in particular where I felt there was a spirit, and I stayed behind as the rest of the group moved on to see what would happen. The spirit was definitely female, and seemed to be some kind of servant. She was very nervous about what I was doing in there. I think she was worried I was going to disturb something. She seemed to be trying to get a truck and luggage together for a trip of some kind. I took several photographs during our exchange and this is the only one that had anything unusual in it.

The Library

Another area of interest was the library, where I sensed the presence of a man who was smoking and relaxing. Research of the house and its history revealed that over the years many people have claimed to have experienced the ghost of a man in the library. Tradition holds that it's Jacob. Other reports I have heard from the library were of phantom tobacco smoke.

A Maid and Child

There have also been sightings of a ghostly maid. Legend says she fell down the steps and died.

One spirit that I later read about but did not experience was that of Mary, a playful little girl ghost. She is most often seen in the nursery and has even been known to spell her name out in the blocks there. I wondered if she ever spelled her name out on the old Ouija Board ® that is on display in that location. It was great to see the Ouija Board® in with the toys, as it was originally intended as a children's toy and would have been in the nursery.

Nemacolin Castle
Brashear and Front Streets
Brownsville, PA 15147
www.nemacolincastle.org

A misty shape appeared in this photo of the attic.
(Most evident on the right side of the photo.)

Graeme Park - Horsham

It was a beautiful fall day when I went to meet the ghostly residents of Graeme Park. Traffic constantly flew by on the main road, but it was still easy to imagine how things were in the late 1700s when this was Elizabeth Graeme-Fergusson's home. Back then, this was an isolated property, about thirty miles from the city and any kind of civilization.

The house dates from 1722 and was the home of the then provincial governor, Sir William Keith. He named it "Fountain Low." Unfortunately, not long after his lovely home was finished, Sir Keith fell out with the powers that be (The Penns) and was forced to give up his governorship. In 1739, it was purchased by Dr. Thomas Graeme, who was married to Ann Diggs, the governor's stepdaughter. He wanted to use it as a summer residence. The primary residence of the family was Carpenter's Mansion in the 600 block of Chestnut Street in Philadelphia.

Dr. Graeme enjoyed entertaining in a way that reflected his high position in society, so the estate was the scene of many parties. When the good doctor died, the estate was left to his youngest daughter, Elizabeth. Elizabeth was a very educated and refined lady for her time.

She fell in love with William Franklin (son of the famous Benjamin), but the romance did not work out. She then met and married a Scottish man named Henry Hugh Fergusson. He fought with the British during the American Revolution, so during the war, he spent little time with his wife and afterwards the climate was such that he left with the British troops after the surrender.

Their property was seized by the Americans as was all property of traitors, and its furnishings were sold at public auction. Elizabeth had managed to hold on to a few influential and wealthy friends, and they helped her get Graeme Park back. She lived there with her niece until 1795. Her poor health and financial problems led to her sale of the property to her niece's husband.

That isolation must have been difficult for Elizabeth, who had been debuted into society, well-educated, traveled to Europe, and associated with such notables as Benjamin West and Dr. Benjamin Rush. She passed away at the home of a friend, not far from Graeme Park, in 1801 and shortly after, the Graeme Park property was sold to the Penrose family.

The hallway to Elizabeth's room.

Elizabeth Remains

In 1920, Mr. Welsh Strawbridge purchased the house and when he married Margaret Eli Marshall in 1922, they moved in. Mrs. Strawbridge is the first person who experienced the ghost of Elizabeth. She said she heard the rustling of skirts in the house, similar to the sound that a long, full dress would have made.

Since then, Elizabeth has been sighted inside the house that went from a summer home to her permanent residence after the American Revolution. Her presence has been associated with the smell of strong lavender perfume and disembodied footsteps on the main staircase.

As I sat listening to the kind and knowledgeable ladies of the Graeme Park Friends Society, my attention was drawn to the portrait of a sad young woman that seemed to look down on us.

"That's Elizabeth," they said as they noticed where my gaze had fallen.

"Oh," I replied, "Did she have children?"

I was not sure why I asked that. I felt that the woman in the portrait was so sad and that it had some connection with children. They said that she had not had any children. I thought perhaps that was why she was sad, but had a nagging feeling there was more to that story.

The master bedroom was Dr. Graeme's room, and here some guides and guests have smelled pipe smoke. This is believed to be the presence of Elizabeth's father, Dr. Graeme. My feeling as we entered the room was that he liked his privacy. I was thinking he preferred for guests to be announced.

When we entered Elizabeth's room, the impression I got was again that Elizabeth was sad. I felt that she had a lot of regrets and made many bad choices. She didn't know why she did some of the things she did; in thinking back, they were mistakes. She felt she may have had bad luck or a curse on her somehow.

I felt very strongly that Elizabeth still lingered at her home, even though it would seem to me that the summer home would have been an unhappy reminder of her younger, happier days. Elizabeth's main concern that I picked up on was that people were talking about her. Her husband, Henry, was eleven years younger than she was and she had married him in secret. In addition, she is said to have tripped over a tombstone as she left the churchyard the day of her wedding. Perhaps this is the source of what I picked up on when I felt that she thought she may have been cursed with bad luck. Her father never even knew about it because he had died before she could tell him.

Henry was described as very charming and literate, so it is likely that Elizabeth was attracted to and affectionate towards him. Letters that were written between them indicate a great deal of affection, but the marriage did not result in a *happily ever after* for them. They were not together very much, due to Henry serving on the side of the British in the War for Independence. This made it impossible for him to stay after the war and caused Elizabeth to lose her property. When she married Fergusson, the title to the property reverted to him, and the property was seized as was property of other British supporters. There were also allegations that Henry had had an affair – a child born to her sister's servant who was even said to have been fathered by him. Elizabeth spent the last twenty-five years of her life obsessed with finding out the truth about this matter.

This, I believe, is why Elizabeth was so concerned about being gossiped about. My tour guide confirmed that the situation with the illegitimate child did cause Elizabeth much distress, to the point where she felt she could not even go out in public. He wrote letters to her, asking her to believe that he had not been unfaithful, but doubts overshadowed her feelings for him and she was not able to get past it.

Skeptics Beware

Are Elizabeth and her father the only ghosts at Graeme Park? Some visitors have heard the laughter of children, and one incident in particular leads me to believe there may be some ghostly children there. The incident involved the most skeptical person I talked to at Graeme Park, which made it all the more interesting.

There is a closet in what was the children's room where the fire extinguishers are kept. There is a pin inside the closet that allows the closet to be locked from the inside by sliding the pin into a hole on the floor.

One day when the tour guide went in to open the house, she went to get the fire extinguisher and could not get the closet open. She felt under the door and realized the pin was slid into the hole, locking the closet from the inside. It stayed locked for a couple of weeks and then suddenly, one day, it was unlocked. This was more mystifying than it being locked, because while one may explain away it being locked as the bolt just happening to have slipped into the hole, it was difficult to explain how the same bolt, unreachable from the outside, had now slid up, to the left, and back onto the hook it normally sits on without the help of someone's hand. I asked her what her explanation for this was and she replied that she did not have an explanation for this event.

Locked In

Another interesting feature in the house is the heavy latches on the outside of the bedroom doors upstairs. Each door has one, and they seem designed to keep someone in rather than out.

These hook latches are believed to date from the time when "Aunt Polly" lived here. Aunt Polly lived there during the time the Penrose family owned the property and was either a relative of the Penroses or a member of the community. She was described as "crazy." It is unclear from the description whether she was mentally ill or developmentally delayed. She was allowed to just live in the house.

One of the stories claimed that she routinely fished for chickens in the pond. The locks were possibly a way of protecting her by confining her to one area if she was having a bad spell. The ghost of Aunt Polly is not believed to be among the spectral inhabitants of Graeme Park, but is an interesting and creepy part of its history.

This latch seems more designed to keep someone in the room.

Battery Drains

As I walked through the house with my Mel Meter, which is an electronic device that measures the electromagnetic field levels and ambient temperature, I experienced a complete battery drain on the meter. A brand new nine volt battery went from 100 percent to nothing in the space of about 45 minutes. When a local news network was filming a segment at Graeme Park, the camera battery, which had been at 80 percent, suddenly was completely depleted and they had to use a backup battery. According to the Friends, electrical disturbances are common at Graeme Park. The alarms, which have motion detectors, routinely cannot be set due to electrical malfunctions and sometimes due to detected movement in Elizabeth's bedroom. If you go to Graeme Park, make sure you bring extra batteries!

As I left the mansion that day, I couldn't help but look back. The feeling that someone was watching me from the windows as I walked away was overwhelming. I glanced back and took a few photos that revealed nothing unusual, but that feeling was there. Before I got in my car I gave Elizabeth a quick wave goodbye. I hope she knows I wish her well.

Graeme Park
859 County Line Road
Horsham, PA 19044
215-343-0965
http://www.ushistory.org/graeme/index.htm

Creepy Cafes and Restaurants

If we are able to return after death to places we loved in life, then the fact that many restaurants seem to be haunted should come as no surprise. The four restaurants featured here are historic as well, so there are many reasons to think that cold spot you pass as you take your favorite chair may be a patron from the past.

Lamb Tavern - Springfield

The Lamb Tavern is one of my favorite places to have meetings and also just for lunch or dinner with friends. It has been a Springfield landmark since 1808, when a man named Eamor Eachus moved to a house near the Springfield Friends Quaker Meeting House and applied for a license to operate a public house. He named the tavern "The Three Tuns." It quickly became a popular place with locals and travelers; playing host to livestock auctions, produce sales, and was a militia meeting place and recruiting point.

At this time, there was another tavern in Springfield called "The Lamb." When that original Lamb Tavern ceased business in 1835, the owner of the Three Tuns decided to change the name of his establishment to The Lamb. All was well until 1881, when then owner Malachi Sloan died and one of the provisions of his will was that the Lamb no longer operate as a hotel. It is a mystery why he felt so strongly about this. My feeling is that Mr. Sloan may have had some experience with or knowledge of some of the unseen residents there. His wish was only granted for about fourteen years; by 1895 the Lamb was back in business.

Upper Floor Haunts

The upper floors of the restaurant, which used to be the guest rooms, are now used for storage. Oddly, when we asked about access to the fourth floor we were told there wasn't one, even though we could clearly see fourth floor windows with curtains on them from the outside of the building!

The manager declined to accompany us to the third floor. She remained at the bottom of the staircase as we explored the storage rooms. I turned left at the top of the stairs and headed towards the window. A black shadowy form dashed across the hallway, right in my path. I jumped back and called out in alarm. The team members who accompanied me rushed over to see what had happened. As I began explaining what I had seen, the manager called up from the bottom of the stairs.

"Is everything all right?" she asked.

"Yes, why don't you come up and see?" I responded.

She declined and we continued to explore the rooms. The shadowy figure did not appear again, but when we crossed the landing to have a look at the rooms to the right of the stairs, I began to make out a low whispery moaning sound. I stopped walking and asked the person next to me if they heard anything. She admitted she heard something, but wasn't sure what it was. I continued into the room, in search of the source of the sounds.

There was a presence in the room that was discernible as I passed the threshold. There seemed to be two men in the room and they gave the impression of pleading for water. They were burning up with some kind of fever and had been abandoned there. I was not able to get a clear picture of what year it was or exactly what the nature of their illness could be. I felt that they died there, in delirium, and were not aware how much time had passed or that they were dead.

The Tavern no longer has rooms for rent, but you can always visit the spirits here by making a dinner or lunch reservation.

This view of Lamb Tavern clearly shows a fourth story.

Lamb Tavern
865 West Springfield Road
Springfield, PA 19064
(610) 544-3300
www.lambtavern.com

Lardin House - Masontown

Now a nicely decorated restaurant, Lardin House was built in 1878 as a farmhouse. The property, however, has been inhabited since at least 1769, when John Harrison built a small building on the property that for some unknown reason he called "Poor's Choice." According to the owner, there have been two paranormal investigation teams there to try and document some of the activity reported, but they did not have much luck in doing so. The owners are convinced the place is haunted and have heard many accounts from frequent visitors who validate their feelings of not being alone at the property. It's not clear who might haunt the place and rumors abound about murders, burial grounds, the Underground Railroad, and shackles on the basement walls.

When I arrived at the Lardin House, I was surprised to see such an impressive house. The interior is just as impressive as the outside and contains many period antiques and interesting architectural details that show how the house evolved over the years into the eighteen-room mansion it is today. The mansion was always a private home until 1991, when it first became a restaurant.

The Lardin House Inn still resembles the home it was.

Watched

We had a seat in the bar area while we waited for Louise Blaker, one of the owners, to give us a tour. My attention was continually drawn to the hallway and the inside front door of the house as I was positive someone kept walking past the front door. As I stood in the doorway and watched, I became more convinced that there was something unseen there. Having stood in the doorway to "watch," I now felt as if I was the one *being* watched!

Louise came back into the room and we started the tour. I asked Louise about the hallway near the front door, as I had been picking up on the spirit of a woman there. She was the one who was pacing back and forth. At this time, the room to the left of the front door was occupied by a group of ladies having their weekly meeting. Louise showed us that room first and mentioned that one of the previous owners had actually died in that room. I asked if he had died after an illness and she confirmed that he had. My feeling was that the woman was a family member who was taking care of him, and that was why she was pacing. The feeling I had was more that she was a daughter than his wife.

Helpful Spirits

The tour then led us through the other dining room and back towards the kitchen and up the stairs, which Louise explained were points of activity. One experience that they shared with me was told to them by a bride who had been married in the Lardin House.

She and her party had dressed upstairs, and at the appointed time, she made her entrance by going down the front stairs in her gown. As she descended the stairs, she felt someone unseen lift the back hem of her dress so it wouldn't drag on the stairs. I wondered if the wedding photographer picked up anything on those photos! I felt strongly that this was the spirit of a woman. Lifting the hem of a dress to protect it doesn't sound like something a man would do.

We noted an area upstairs above the current kitchen where there seemed to be a protective spirit. When I asked about this, the owner remarked that, at one time, there had been a fire there, and showed us the char marks. Perhaps this explains why the ghost has been known to react strongly to cigars left smoldering in ashtrays. On one occasion, someone lit up a cigar in the bar area and put it down in the ashtray. The ashtray then split violently in two, right in front of the smoker and the bartender.

Other Strange Things

The current owners say they have never seen or experienced any of the ghosts that reportedly inhabit the Lardin House, but when they moved there, he noticed a change in his dog's behavior. While they were inside the Lardin House the dog refused to leave his side. The dog also refused to go onto the third floor and had to be dragged up there.

The previous owners, when asked, told the current owners that they heard chains in the basement. When they had purchased the house, there were metal rings embedded in the walls of one basement room with shackles still attached to some of them. Another interesting feature was that there was a tunnel, now closed off and filled in, that led from one section of the basement that came out by the springhouse. Whether this tunnel was connected to the presence of the shackles is unknown. It is likely the tunnel served many purposes and was mainly functional and provided a sheltered path to the springhouse during the winter. It was likely then used for a variety of purposes. The owners said that the property owners first owned slaves and then became involved with the Underground Railroad.

Interestingly, Louise, one of the current owners, will not go into the basement. Her reason was "It's too creepy," although she said that she has never experienced anything unusual down there.

The outside of the house is just as interesting as the inside. There is an old springhouse, and acres of land to explore. Many people, me included, have reported feeling of being watched from the front of the house as they walked outside. One group of Civil war re-enactors reported seeing a Civil War era family sitting on the front porch as they camped out front.

Disturbed Burial Ground

The owner was told that there is a Native American site as well as a slave burial ground somewhere on the property. He has not been able to locate either place yet, but it is known that when the highway was built in the 1960s some human remains were found and moved. We were unable to find where these remains were moved to, but a disturbed gravesite can be the trigger for paranormal activity.

The Native American burial ground was said to be marked by five large stones; four at the corners and one on the center. It is said that Ben Lardin did not allow anyone to go back there and his cows refused to graze within the area marked by the stones. When we began talking about the Native American burial site and the stones, the Mel Meter EMF suddenly went up to 2.3 MG. Although this could have been caused by a natural surge, we also wondered if perhaps we had stirred up some energy with our discussion. Maybe it was Ben Lardin, still wanting to keep people away from that area.

Whether it is Ben Lardin still trying to protect the property, or a woman lifting a hem, watching over her sick father, and making sure the house doesn't catch fire again, the ghosts here are very protective and vigilant, still watching over their big, beautiful house in the scenic countryside of Fayette County.

Lardin House
1892 McClellandtown Road
Masontown, PA 15461
(724) 583-8310
www.lardinhouseinn.com

One of the owners described the basement as "too creepy" to enter.

The General Lafayette Inn - Lafayette Hills

After hearing rumors for years that this place was haunted, I decided to set up a meet-up for potential members there. The dinner was delicious, but paranormally uneventful. Afterwards, the staff allowed us to explore the building a little. I was unsure of who or what was supposed to happen there. The staff didn't seem to know either, so off we went up the stairs to the private dining rooms.

There was one room that caught my attention right away. As soon as I stepped in, I was uncomfortable. The presence of a woman was coming through very strongly for me. There were two other ladies at the meeting that I felt had the ability to see or sense spirits, so I asked them to accompany me into the room.

Being inexplicably locked in this room was a disturbing experience.

Locked In – Again

There was such an eerie, uncomfortable feeling in there. One of the other ladies put her hand to her throat and seemed to be picking up on what I was seeing. I was seeing a woman in great distress. She was screaming, crying and in great fear of someone. I felt that we would have better luck communicating with her if there were no men in the room, and we shut off the light and closed the door while remaining inside.

We did this, but nothing happened. After a while of waiting we decided to leave the room, but when I turned the knob, it was locked. We looked for a lock, but didn't see any locking mechanism, so we started banging on the door. Just when panic started to set in, a staff person heard us and opened the door from the outside. He seemed surprised that we were locked in and asked us how it happened. We related exactly what we had done and he glanced at the doorknob and then back at us.

"There's no lock on that door. You just didn't push hard enough."

Is he kidding? I thought to myself. All three of us had tried to open that door, separately and together, with no luck. We headed downstairs to leave and had chalked up the whole experience to an old door with a funky knob. I happened to see a paper on the history of the inn on a table as we left, so I grabbed one and started reading it as we walked towards the car.

I was surprised to see that one of the ghosts listed there was of a woman who was murdered. I have been unable to find out any more information about this woman. Most telling was farther down in the paragraph, "being unable to open an unlock-able door can be a frightening experience."

When the Inn changed ownership we went back to see if the new owners experienced anything. To our surprise the little room that we had been locked in was now a storage area and was no longer used!

The events reported at the inn are typical of most haunted places. Doors open and shut by themselves and footsteps are heard when there is no one about. The doorknob to the upstairs office has been known to rattle on its own, too. There were also reports of an empty chair that could not be moved until it was "ready" to, and another report of a chair spinning on one leg.

The other ghosts at the inn are that of a father and son, who have been seen outside the inn. They are assumed to have been one-time caretakers of the property.

The room is currently used for storage.

As we were leaving the inn that night, I noticed a cemetery right behind the parking lot. I wondered if this had anything to do with the paranormal activity there. After a subsequent visit to the inn, we decided to walk over to the cemetery and see if anything might be relevant to the haunting at the inn. We didn't see or experience anything that night, so I decided to do some research on the area.

I had barely started looking up the history when my phone rang. It was Bill, one of our group members.

"Remember that restaurant we were at in Lafayette Hills?" he asked

"Of course," I replied, "I am trying to find out the history of the place.

"Well, my friend owns a studio across the street and they say it is haunted, too." [Lafayette Hills Studio]

We set up a time to go to the studio and check it out. We toured the entire studio and when we were in the basement. I thought I was picking up on some Underground Railroad activity. The owner said the building wasn't that old and he wasn't sure of the history other than that it used to be the fire house. Not much happened until Bill and I were alone in the one studio, transferring audio files. I saw a globe of light floating by the curtain. When I called Bill's attention to it, he was intrigued. We went in to the other studio to get someone else to come in and see what we were seeing. Maybe there was an explanation.

The studio owner just stared at what we were pointing at. He didn't say anything. After a few minutes the light went away. As we were packing up our recording equipment, I saw a face peek through the curtain.

Bill and the owner didn't see the face, but we waited a few more minutes to see if anything else would happen. Nothing did, so we left for the night.

We had moved on to other places and projects when the studio owner called Bill one night. The strangest thing had happened. They were doing a photo shoot with a small child, and during the shoot they noticed that the child kept looking over to the curtain, pointing and laughing at seemingly nothing. The child's behavior reminded him that I had seen a face there, so he had to call us. Additionally, he said that he had seen the light that night, but he didn't know what to say or think about it, so he didn't say anything!

Research on the inn and the area revealed that the first inn on the property was built in 1732. It was known as the "Three Tuns" This makes it one of the oldest in the United States. The inn predates the adjacent church and cemetery, which were founded in 1752. The inn was almost fifty years old when the American Revolution arrived on its doorstep.

The British had captured Philadelphia the previous fall, after the Battle of Germantown. On May 18, 1778, General Washington sent General Lafayette and over 2,000 men from their encampment at Valley Forge over to Barren Hill, which we now know as Lafayette Hills, to spy on the British troop movements. The British soon learned of the plan and sent their troops to surround Lafayette and his men.

On May 19th, Lafayette found out that "the British were coming," and he needed a plan. He left some men and cannons at St. Peter's Church to engage the British and act as decoys while the rest of them escaped. The ruse worked and on the 22nd Lafayette was back at Barren Hill, spying on the British until June 19th, when they were met by General Washington, and joined him as he marched to glory at Monmouth, New Jersey.

While Lafayette was camped there, it is believed that General William Smallwood and General William Hull had their headquarters in the Three Tuns. The whole hillside, including the property of the inn, the church, the studio, and Brittingham's next door, all saw the Battle of Barren Hill. Are the echoes of this long-ago battle still heard today? Events would seem to indicate that at least some of these unexplained events have their roots there.

The General Lafayette Inn
646 Germantown Pike
Lafayette Hills, PA 19444
(610) 941-0600
www.generallafayetteinn.com

BRITTINGHAM'S - LAFAYETTE HILLS

Brittingham's was built in 1743 as an inn that offered rest, drink, and companionship to those traveling the Germantown Pike. The inn was patronized by Lafayette's men when they camped there before and after the Battle of Barren Hill.

According to the Inn's website, "local residents told of seeing the initials of many of Lafayette's men inscribed in the stone walls of the root cellar under the Inn. Entrance to the 'cave' was from the outside of the building down a twenty foot circular staircase, now sealed shut."[19] It appears that Brittingham's was the place where the enlisted men gathered, while the officers gravitated to the General Lafayette.

Brittingham's website also states that "prior to and during the Civil War, the Inn was used as an 'Underground Railroad'"[20]. A tunnel ran from the Inn to the General Lafayette Hotel, then to St. Peter's Cemetery. I felt validated about my Underground Railroad impressions from the studio basement.

Tunnels under this bar and restaurant were used in the Underground Railroad.

The Devil Made Them Do It

Around 1900, there was a gambling parlor for men on the first floor with music and dancing on the third floor. This is when the first ghost stories began circulating about Brittingham's. Locals swore that they had seen the devil peering in the windows whenever any card playing was going on. I think this was most likely a turn of the twentieth century urban legend, told to try and keep people from the "sin" of gambling. So, the devil doesn't peer in the windows at the patrons, but there have been some unexplained happenings in the bar area.

The previous owners of Brittingham's were navy veterans and proud of it. They had hung their caps from two hooks up above the bar. One busy weekend night, both caps suddenly flew off the hooks and across the bar to land on the floor. The employees and patrons sat in stunned silence for a minute, but when nothing else happened they continued on with their evening. Was a ghostly Army veteran expressing his displeasure that the Navy had taken over their tavern?

More recently the bartenders have seen a young man with dark hair, dressed in a dark short and khaki trousers pass the bar as if he were walking towards the men's room. They never see him come in or sit down. He just appears suddenly, passes the far section of the bar, and disappears and he reaches the end of the bar. He just started appearing about five years ago. In the beginning, his appearances were very frequent, but have now become less so. The theory on his identity is that he is likely a patron from recent years who passed away suddenly and is just stopping by as he did in life at one of his local bars.

Brittingham's Irish Pub and Restaurant
640 East Germantown Pike
Lafayette Hill, PA 19444
(610) 828-7351
www.brittinghams.com

Spooky Cemeteries

Older cemeteries seem to have a strange energy. As you walk among the headstones, you catch yourself constantly looking over your shoulder. Many of these old cemetery sites were chosen because they had that eerie kind of energy. Legends spring up around the cemeteries or around unusual markers as we attempt to explain the feelings of unease we have there.

The Gnaden Huetten Massacre - Lehighton

I was directed to this site by another paranormal investigator. If he hadn't told me about it, I doubt I would ever have discovered it on my own, as the local residents do not seem to know much about it and are reluctant to give directions. The area is rural and residential. Since I was not a local, I stood out to begin with. When I started asking about the ghosts, I could feel the suspicion building in the people I asked. One of them even asked me, "Why would you want to go stirring that stuff up?"

Armed with the sketchy description from my paranormal buddy, a friend and I headed off down the roads of Lehighton. I saw the plaque right away. It was very creepy looking. The plaque is at the intersection of two roads and marks the site of a Moravian Mission-ary settlement. The sign reads, "This was the first settlement in Carbon County, founded in 1746. On the night of that fateful day in November of 1755, the settlement was attacked by the Shawnees Indians. Eleven people lost their lives, five of whom died in the flames of their house. Their remains are buried in the Lehighton Cemetery on the hill to the north."

As I stood reading the plaque, I heard the sound of children play-ing not far behind me. I turned and the cemetery was right there, across the street from a row of houses. Legend has it that the massacred missionaries who are buried under the monument do not really rest there. Instead, their shadowy forms leave the grave and wander around the cemetery and the massacre site at night. The local people didn't seem too concerned about ghosts. The cemetery apparently serves as a playground for the children that live near there.

The Grave

We turned in to the graveyard just as the sun was going down. This was not the best time of day and season to explore this site. We got out of the car and were immediately surrounded by what seemed like every lightning bug and mosquito in Pennsylvania. Although I definitely felt a presence there begging for a story to be told, I quickly realized that any kind of serious investigation would have to wait for cooler weather. With the insect population multiplying exponentially, we fled and left them to it. Unfortunately, I was unable to get back to the grave on that trip.

As we drove away from the cemetery into the growing darkness, I could not shake the feeling that there was more to this story than what was on the plaque. When I got back home I began hitting the books and the internet for more information.

The Missionaries

Count Nickolas Ludwig Von Zinzendorf founded this settlement in 1746, with settlers from an established Moravian Mission community at Bethlehem, Pennsylvania. The Moravians also had established communities at Nazareth and Lititz, Pennsyl-vania. The new settlement, which was located in the Mahoning Valley in the area currently known as Lehigh-ton, was the first white settlement in the area. According to records of the Moravian Mission, the settlement was also inhabited by many Native Americans, who, together with the white missionary families, comprised

The actual site of the settlement and the massacre is marked by this sign.

Site Of The
Gnaden Huetten Massacre
November 24, 1755
This was the first settlement in Carbon County, founded in 1746. On the night of that fatal day in 1755 the settlement was attacked by the Shawnees Indians. Eleven people lost their lives, 5 of whom died in the flames of their house. Their remains are buried in the Lehighton Cemetery on the hill to the north.

The mass grave of the Moravian missionaries.
Photo courtesy of Rich Hickman.

the "congregation of gnadenhuetten." Gnaden Huetten means "huts of grace." The Native American residents of this settlement worshipped and celebrated with the white missionaries and they farmed their own land.

The other tribes in the area did not like the idea of Indians and white settlers living together. The tribes became more agitated when, as a result of the Albany Congress in 1754, their land and hospitality was further imposed upon. As a result of this land purchase of the Albany Congress, the Indians allied with the French, who were beginning their preparations for the French and Indian Wars. Many frontier settlements were ravaged during this time, and I believe that this settlement was a victim of this period of unrest between the various groups inhabiting the region.

Then I ran into some conflicting information. The monument in the cemetery lists the eleven victims described on the sign. They all had German names, so were likely the missionaries. A *Pocono Record* article published on September 29, 1998, stated that the settlement was actually raided by white men in retaliation for an Indian raid, and that a lot of Delaware Indians were murdered there. The article referred to them as Delaware Indians, but the historical records stated that they were Mohicans. The records of the Moravian Missionaries, which are kept at the University of Maryland Library, record the Indians of Gnaden Huetten being Mohican. This was not necessarily an error, since Delaware is not an Indian word. It is an English word, and was used by the English settlers to describe a number of tribes, including the Lenape and Shawnee. The settlement was most likely raided by the French and the Indians, resulting in deaths of both white missionaries and Indians. I suppose the Indian victims were buried elsewhere without a marker or monument.

A Different Story?

This account was so totally different from the statement on the sign I couldn't believe it. I decided to visit the site again in cooler weather to see if I could get some answers from the source. The presence there at the grave was still there, but seemed fleeting. I was picking up on flames and screaming, but I wasn't seeing very many Native Americans. What was she trying to show me? I began to think about the dates again and the political climate of that time. The people I was seeing were speaking a language I could sort of recognize. Some of the words were French.

I was beginning to think that the settlement was not raided by Native Americans at all. There may have been a few of them there, and they may have known some French words, but I felt strongly that the raiding party that day was made up of quite a few Frenchmen as well, eager to play on tribal rivalries and agitate the English settlers by attacking these outposts under the guise of being part of a Native American tribe.

This theory was given further support when I was contacted by a fellow researcher who had read my account online. She provided me with a contemporary account of the massacre.

"There were fifteen persons in the dwelling-house on that fatal night. One man had been returning from locking up the meeting house when he was met by another resident who breathlessly told him they were under attack by Twelve Shawanese painted for war."[21] He had just escaped certain death by jumping out of a window. They decided it would be better to run and get help than try to confront the raiding party.

The residents, who consisted of families of men, women, children, and infants, barricaded themselves in an attic room. When the raiders couldn't force the door, they set building on fire. Some were able to escape by making a successful leap from the burning structure only to be shot and scalped as they tried to flee.

In a book called *History of the Lehigh Valley* by M.S. Henry and published 1860...there is a reprint of a written account of what happened that night. In the letter, an eyewitness claims to have seen a member in the group of natives that attacked the home dressed in a "French Patch Coat"[22]. If this was not a Frenchman, he certainly had dealings with one.

Over the years I have added to my research about this massacre and others like it. It is surprising how many of them there are in Pennsylvania. It seemed that usually an old person or small children were left as witnesses to tell the authorities that the atrocities were committed by "Indians." No one was ever held accountable for these deaths. It seems to have been accepted as part of life on the frontier. When I revisit the location where a massacre happened, I am always glad to return home. It just feels like there is some kind of depressing pall over that area. Some of the people who have contacted me about the story seem to think the area is cursed because of the acts committed there. I don't know if it is cursed, but it is definitely haunted.

St. James Episcopal Cemetery - Bristol

This little cemetery on a residential street in Bristol is home to a very strange legend. Rumor has it that if one sits on the "Witch's Chair" at midnight, especially on Halloween, her arms will reach out from the grave to grab whomever is sitting there.

One of the beautiful Victorian monuments at St. James.

The Witch's Chair

The iron chair is right in front of the grave of Merritt P. Wright and his wife, Sarah. The chair reads "Merritt P. Wright" and I have not been able to find out anything about his life or why he would be associated with this witch legend. There are two possibilities that came to mind when I visited the grave.

First of all, there is the chair. While not unusual in cemeteries with graves from the Victorian Era, it is the only chair in this cemetery. It is also a black iron chair, not a stone one, so it stands out. Chairs were used on graves to either give the mourner a place to sit and mourn the person or were placed there as a concrete reminder that from now on their chair will be empty; no one will be able to fill their chair. Since the chair is so unusual looking and is the only one there, it is natural that some stories would attach themselves to it.

The other odd thing is that his wife, Sarah, born in 1851, has a blank square where her date of death should be. It's not that it was left blank, there is a square placed where the date of death should be. This means either she was buried somewhere else or maybe it was in dispute for some reason. This could easily be misinterpreted to have some kind of sinister meaning and is likely the source of the witch stories.

I have been there at midnight on Halloween and at other times. Nothing ever grabbed me when I sat in the chair, nor have I ever felt that the chair was haunted. It is just an unusual feature in that cemetery and an interesting and kind of creepy-looking piece of Victorian mourning memorabilia.

The Witch's Chair.

Holy Cross Cemetery - Yeadon

America's First Serial Killer

I'm not sure how I came across the information, but there it was in a file marked H. H. Holmes. In the folder there was a copy of an article that had appeared in our local paper about how America's first serial killer was buried right up the road in Yeadon, Pennsylvania. One gloomy afternoon we decided to go look for it.

As we passed the cemetery, I realized our task was going to be huge. The cemetery was massive and all we had was a lot number. How were we going to find a single, unmarked grave in this place?

We discussed a strategy as we pulled up in front of the office. Since we had a lot number, we figured that one of us could go into the office and ask for the exact location of the grave of Herman Mudgett. My companion and fellow researcher, Lori, marched up to the door and went in, determined to charm the information out of whoever was in there. Her face when she emerged a few minutes later told me it hadn't worked. It seemed that the archdiocese had forbidden that the location of that particular grave could never be revealed. It was time for Plan B.

Our equipment includes traditional dowsing rods as well as pendulums. These, coupled with our own sensitivity, would hopefully lead us the right way.

There were quite a few groundskeepers around, so it was decided to use a pendulum as that is less obvious than dowsing rods. We walked around for a bit, getting a feel for the energy of the place, and right away we were drawn to one area. Was this it? I got out the pendulum.

A pendulum is basically a pendant suspended on a chain. It is held between the index and middle fingers of the hand and can answer questions or locate hidden objects based on the swings and rotations made by the pendulum. We were going to ask for a direction and follow the swings to get to the gravesite.

The approximate location of the burial.

There was a large depression in the ground with a little spray of white wildflowers in the center. As we stepped onto the area the pendulum began swinging in a wide circle. It began to circle more quickly and I started to feel dizzy and sick to my stomach. When I stepped off the area it all stopped but I felt like I was beginning to get a migraine. We were sure that if this was not the grave, we had certainly located something that deserved more investigation.

H. H. Holmes

Although most of his atrocities he is credited with were committed in his so-called "Murder Castle" in Chicago, Herman Mudgett, aka H. H. Holmes, was imprisoned, executed, and buried in Philadelphia. He experienced a jailhouse conversion to Roman Catholicism and this is why he was buried in Holy Cross Cemetery, but did his soul move on to Purgatory or Heaven as one would expect? Not if one believed the tales of the curse that followed those involved with this execution and burial and the strange events reported by that those who visited his gravesite.

Herman Mudgett was born in 1861 in a small town in New England, where he grew to be an intelligent and attractive medical student with a bright future. He was kicked out of medical school when it was discovered that he was stealing cadavers for use in an insurance fraud scheme. The scheme was that he would purchase insurance for "relatives" and then steal a cadaver and identify it as the deceased relative and collect on the policy. When the fraud was discovered, he moved to Chicago and changed his name to Henry Howard Holmes. He took a position in a pharmacy where he quickly made himself indispensable to Mrs. Holton, who was trying to operate the pharmacy started by her now ailing and infirm husband. When Mr. Holton died, he agreed to purchase the pharmacy. He was unable to keep up with the payments and luckily for him Mrs. Holton conveniently disappeared.

Holmes then moved the business across the road to a building at 63rd and Wallace, which was later called the Murder Castle. The more lurid reports of what went on during the construction and during the time when the missing people were said to have stayed there are largely taken from the testimony of an employee of Mudgett's, Quinlan, who was nearly implicated in the disappearances and suspected murders and was definitely connected indirectly with the murders of the Pietzel girls. The girls' bodies were found in a house owned by one of his wife's relatives. His account, at least to my reckoning must be suspect, especially since shortly after the discovery of some human bones in the basement, the entire Murder Castle was burned in an arson fire.

The Crimes

It wasn't suspicion of murder that cause d Holmes to leave Chicago, but bad debts. He had started his old insurance fraud schemes again and this brought him the attention of detectives employed by the insurance companies. His last scheme, which was set in motion as the fake patent business he had set up on Callowhill Street in Philadelphia had a twist that, when unraveled, ended with Holmes swinging from a noose in Philadelphia. The twist was that the insured person ended up dead under suspicious circumstances. This was Benjamin Pietzel, Holmes' partner in the patent business. A search for missing members of the Pietzel family turned up more bodies.

He was arrested for insurance fraud and held in Moyamensing Prison. It must be noted at this time that to his death he denied any part in the murder of the Pietzel family and all of the others he was accused of. According to contemporary newspaper accounts, his "last words were a denial of any crimes except the deaths of two women by malpractice."[25] The two women referred to in his confession were believed to be "Julia Connor of Chicago, who was believed to be murdered with her daughter, and Emily Cigrand of Anderson, Indiana."[26]

Holmes' Criminal History

He had just opened the drug store in Chicago when he met Minnie Williams. According to his account, she fell in love with him and he set up house with her. She owned about $40,000 worth of property in Ft. Worth, Texas. Her sister, Nettie, appeared on the scene and also fell for Holmes, which made Minnie insanely jealous. According to Holmes, Minnie killed Nettie in a jealous rage and he helped her hide the body. He said that they sunk the body in Lake Michigan, by putting it in a trunk loaded with stones. Holmes then claimed he gave her enough money to escape to England.

When questioned about the missing Pietzel children, he claimed that they were in England with a "Miss Williams." The children were later found dead in a Toronto house and Miss Williams never came forward to defend Mr. Holmes. Perhaps she was fearful of being implicated for her part, but more likely she was also dead. Her body has never been recovered. Shortly after her sudden disappearance, the paper trail shows that Holmes took over her Ft. Worth property. It was at this time that Pietzel joined with him. Holmes and Pietzel conspired together to leave Chicago and set up a scheme in Philadelphia.

They had Pietzel insured, and "On Sept. 4 his body was found there, face burned, indications of an explosion around. Death was due to 'congestion of the lungs, caused by inhalation of flames, chloroform, or some poisonous drug.'"[27] His body was identified by his daughter Alice, who was accompanied by Holmes. The insurance company paid the money.

Then the insurance company received a letter from M. C. Hedgepath, a convicted train robber. He said that Holmes had visited him in jail and asked him to recommend a lawyer to help him with insurance fraud. Hedgepath had referred him to one, and for this was to be paid $500. According to Hedgepath, Holmes had not paid him.

When questioned, Holmes admitted to insurance fraud, but said Pietzel was alive and well and living with three of his children in South America. The body they found in the business on Callowhill Street was a cadaver. Further questioning induced him to admit that the body was Pietzel's, but Holmes claimed he had committed suicide.

The authorities then tried to locate the three youngest Pietzel children, who Mrs. Pietzel claimed were traveling with Holmes. In fact, the three children, Howard, Nettie, and Alice were dead. The bodies of Alice and Nettie were found in a trunk in Toronto. Coincidentally, this house was owned by a relative of a friend of Holmes' janitor at the "Murder Castle" property. The body of Howard was discovered near a house in Indianapolis.

The janitor, Patrick Quinlan, his wife, and their friend, Mrs. Doyle – the one whose relative owned the Toronto house – were questioned at length by the police in connection with the Pietzel murders, the disappearances of the Williams sisters, and the disappearance of Julia Conner and Emily Cigrand. It was discovered that Holmes had insured Quinlan's own daughter, Cora, for $1,000.

At the time, the police felt that "Quinlan made many contradictory and improbable statements"[28] and was likely withholding information. "Mrs. Quinlan was also questioned at length, as was one of her friends, a Mrs. W. L. Doyle. Mrs. Doyle's aunt was the owner of the house where the two Pietzel children were found dead. She claimed that her aunt had rented the house to them."[29]

They were all questioned about the human remains found in the basement of the 63rd Street "Murder Castle," and less than three weeks later the building was set on fire. Witnesses reported that two men had entered the building around 8 or 9 p.m. and were seen exiting a short time later. A partially full can of gasoline was found under the remains of a second floor stairway. An explosion was also reported by some witnesses.

Much has been made of Holmes' supposed jailhouse confession, in which he claimed to have murdered at least twenty people. "The 'confession' lacks one essential qualification – it is untrue."[30] Indeed, "his confession… was disproved when several of the victims were proven to be alive."[31] Holmes' spiritual advisor and the Superintendent of the Prison swore that no one could have entered the prison to talk with Holmes without their knowledge and every piece of mail that has come from or to Holmes was examined by authorities.

To the end, Holmes denied guilt of any murder except the deaths of two women by malpractice. He vehemently denied being responsible for the deaths of any member of the Pietzel family, especially Benjamin Pietzel. The two women referred to in his confession were believed to be Julia Connor of Chicago, who was believed to be murdered with her daughter, and Emily Cigrand of Anderson, Indiana.

He was hanged at the prison on May 27, 1896. Instead of the drop killing him instantly, it took more than ten minutes to slowly strangle. He had left detailed and odd instructions for his burial, likely based on his fear of his corpse being abused.

His instructions, which were carried out by the undertaker, were that his coffin be filled halfway with concrete, his body placed in the wet concrete and then the coffin topped off with more concrete after his face was covered with a cloth. The coffin was then to be buried in a ten-foot deep, double-wide grave. Perhaps because of the weight of the concrete-filled coffin, it accidentally flipped over as they were lowering it into the hole. This resulted in him being buried face down, something that many traditions believe causes the person's spirit to be trapped in the grave.

Another theory about ghosts is that if a person is killed unjustly, his or her spirit may linger to try and carry out the justice they were denied. This could be the case here, especially if as I suspect, the Quinlans were at least as guilty, if not more so, than Holmes.

One of the beautiful graves near
the burial site of a serial killer.

The Curse

The turning of the coffin is what began the rumors of the curse. It is thought by some that the spirit of Herman Mudgett reaches out from beyond death to curse the living.

In early 1910, Marion Hedgepeth, the man who had informed police of Holmes' fraud scheme and caused the opening of the investigation that uncovered Homes' dark deeds was shot by police during a robbery. Not much was made of this until four years later when the *Chicago Tribune* reported the suicide of Pat Quinlan. Mr. Quinlan had poisoned himself because he was haunted by strange dreams and visions that kept him from sleeping.

Author of *The Devil in the White City*, Erik Larsen, reported that as he stood in Holy Cross Cemetery, gazing on the plot of ground he believed contained Holmes' remains, a bolt of lightning struck the ground. In the article that started me on my own quest for the final resting place, the reporter said that when the photographer tried to take a photo of the burial site, his camera shutter jammed.

As we stood on what we believed to be the grave and discussed whether we had really located it or not, I felt a squirmy feeling under my shoes as if I were standing on a pile of worms. I looked down. I saw nothing but grass. My companion shifted a little and looked very uncomfortable.

"What's wrong," I asked her.

"Well, right as were wondering aloud if this was the grave or not, I swear I felt a bang under my foot, like someone was pounding on something under the ground. As we left we noticed that the area of this grave of a murderer, whose victims are said to have included many young children, was surrounded by the graves of a number of young children.

When we walked back towards the car, we crossed ourselves with holy water and said aloud, "We are leaving now and you may not follow us. You must stay here where you belong."

Creepy Colleges and Universities

Stories about haunted colleges go back as far as colleges themselves, and it's not hard to understand why. Between the young imaginations and anxiety of being on your own to the old feel of the buildings, to the use of drugs and day to day drama, colleges and universities often provide a ready source of excess energy for spirits to manifest. Late nights away from home provide the ideal environment for sharing some of these stories with others. Are these just stories made up to scare incoming and impressionable freshmen or is there some substance to these spooky tales? The following entries were selected because they are real events experienced and reported by people who have no explanation for what they experienced.

Bucks County Community College - Newtown

When talking about haunted places in Bucks County, the campus of the community college is nearly always mentioned, and not just by alumni. It seems that most people in the community and the area have heard accounts of the ghost of Tyler Hall.

The ghost of a woman has been seen in Tyler Hall on the campus. The identity of the ghost is believed to be Stella Tyler, who was a former resident, administrator and the building's namesake. The campus is on what was once the estate of George and Stella Tyler, so it makes sense that she would not want to leave her beautiful estate.

Less well known is the ghost of a man who stalks the campus. I first heard about him from a friend of mine who had attended classes there in the late 1970s. She said that she and a group of friends were sitting in the Tyler Gardens. As they sat, relaxing and talking, they all saw a man come through the back entrance of the garden up towards them. All of a sudden, he just wasn't there anymore.

She described him as having longer hair, and he looked a little scruffy. This being the late 1970s, his appearance did not seem out of place for the time. It was when he suddenly vanished they all seemed to agree that there was something odd about him.

I met a few other people who attended BCCC recently. I asked them about the ghosts there and they all admitted that some of the old buildings seem very spooky. One person, though, came back to talk to me at a later date about her experiences there.

"Remember when you asked us about ghosts at Bucks?"

"Of course," I prompted her.

"Well, I never saw that lady ghost, but one day when I was sitting in the garden sketching, I looked up and saw this strange-looking guy that was just there. I mean, when you are sketching, you are looking up and

Bucks County Community College grounds are still tended by a ghostly gardener.

down. It isn't like I would have missed him coming in. When I saw him he really gave me a creepy feeling, like he didn't want me there. I started to get my things together and all of a sudden he just wasn't there anymore. I didn't say anything the other night because I didn't want anyone to laugh at me," she confessed.

I shared the story that my other friend had told me about the group of them that saw a man, omitting the description.

"So, what did he look like?" I asked.

She answered, "You know it is funny. Normally I really notice details because I like to draw, but he was funny. I couldn't seem to get a clear image of his face, just an impression of long hair and kind of dirty clothes."

I nodded and told her that was very similar to the description the others had given, although they hadn't experienced the negative feeling from him that she had.

So who is he? Most likely he is a gardener that used to work there. That would explain the dirty clothes.

The University's student center, Walton Hall, was once the main building of a forty-acre estate and was called Walmarthon. Walmarthon was the home of a leather manufacturer named Charles S. Walton. The name "Walmarthon" was a combination of the name Walton and his wife, Martha's, first name. The original estate was a majestic forty acres and included "a small log, a large greenhouse, a seven-car garage, a three-horse stable, a springhouse complete with a water wheel, and a large gate lodge."[32] There was even a lake called Willow Lake. Wayne and the Main Line were customary places for wealthy Philadelphians to build summer homes where they could escape from the heat of the city.

The Walton family owned the estate until 1935 and hosted a harvest home fete there in 1912 and a silent movie shoot there in 1918. In 1935, the estate was listed for sale, but attracted no interest until 1950, when it was purchased by Eastern Baptist Theological Seminary. In 1952, it became Eastern College and eventually Eastern University.

The Ghosts

Figures in Black

The most common ghost sighting reported here is that of figures dressed in black that disappear right after they are seen. They are most commonly reported near the lake and it is unclear whether they are all the same figure or different entities. Tradition holds that this is the ghost of Charles Walton, roaming his once-beloved estate, but I am not so sure. I feel that this figure may stem from the days of the theological seminary. Although it is possible that it could be Charles Walton, I just don't get that feeling from the place.

Suzanne Walton

There are also rumors of the spirit of a young girl that roams the halls of the dorms and the student center, formerly Walmarthon. This young girl has traditionally been called Suzanne because it is believed that the little girl is the ghost of Suzanne Walton, the Walton's youngest daughter, who died in December of 1929, when she was 7 years old and was buried in West Laurel Hill Cemetery in Philadelphia. It's not clear what she died from, although tradition holds that she was ill.

Walmarthon and one of the lakes.

Let's clear up a little confusion here. Charles S. Walton, Sr. built Walmarthon. He and his wife, Martha, had a son named Charles S. Walton, Jr. Charles Walton, Jr. married May Potts and they had four daughters, the youngest of which was the Suzanne we are referring to. Since this was not his primary residence, it is unlikely that she spent much time there.

She is said to favor the top floor, which is now a storage area. She makes her presence known by walking cross the floors and whimpering and crying behind closed doors in that part of the house. According to an article written by Chelsea Zimmerman for the University newspaper, the top floor rooms contain all kinds of junk, "from bicycle wheels to old yearbooks to the unplugged bell tower bells."[33] The word "Suzy" is scrawled across the walls and there are holes in the floors and walls.

According to the University, the floor has been out of use since the early sixties, but it is unclear why it is not used and why it is not maintained as the rest of the property is. Is the floor closed off because of the ghostly footsteps and disembodied cries of a little girl ghost? It is odd that in an area where space is at a premium, a whole floor of a building is allowed to go to waste.

Doane Hall

Suzy and the mysterious man in black are not the only ghosts as Eastern. Doane Hall is one of the residence halls on the campus and is rumored to be haunted by a female student who committed suicide there. Although rumors of this event are told and retold, I could find no documentation that this death ever occurred.

As you walk around the scenic campus of Eastern University, it is easy to forget that you are on a campus and imagine that you are walking the paths of a country estate on your way to a garden party. As you stroll along, glance at the top floor windows of the main house. You might see the face of a little girl watching you.

Eastern University
1300 Eagle Road
St. David's, PA
www.eastern.edu

WIDENER UNIVERSITY - CHESTER

Widener University was originally the Pennsylvania Military College. The school was relocated to this Chester location in 1862. The campus encompasses many old mansions that were once homes, but have now been converted for use as sororities, fraternities, and office space. Widener is now a coeducational university that offers a wide variety of majors and degree programs.

The Manor

This beautiful mansion was once the home of Jonathan and Louise Woodbridge. It was built as a wedding gift from Jonathan to Louise in 1876, and over the years, was often referred to as "The Louise."

Mrs. Woodbridge was the daughter of a very wealthy family and she was, like many of the wealthy women of her era, very educated and cultured. She sought to bring opportunities for culture to the citizens of her new community and she brought theaters, opera houses, and museums to the city of Chester. Louise loved her beautiful home, with its stained glass windows, numerous fireplaces, and Tiffany chandeliers. She died in the mansion on October 31, 1925 (Halloween!). After the death of her husband in 1935, the "Louise" was given to the city of Chester for use as a home for "genteel ladies of uncertain means."[34] In the 1970s the mansion was purchased by Widener University and today it is still in use by Widener University as the residence for the Phi Sigma Sigma Sorority. It is also believed to be the residence of the ghost of Louise Deshong Woodbridge.

According to what I was told by an employee, Louise stayed in the mansion after her death because she did not want to be parted from her beloved pet dog. It is said that she promised to remain with him, in spirit, as she was dying. Since the start of its use as student housing, there have been consistent reports of footsteps and other unexplained sounds from the room that was once Louise's bedroom. The distinctive sounds of a small dog barking and walking across the floor have also been heard, so it seems that Louise's pet has chosen to remain by her side at the Manor to keep her company in the afterlife.

Louise DeShong remains at her beloved Manor.

Over the years, I have received quite a few reports of paranormal activity from this sorority house. All of the reports have come from residents of the house and employees of the University, and unfortunately they all have requested to remain anonymous. One sorority sister even sent along a few photos they had taken during an event there that showed unusually bright spots, usually referred to as "orbs" and other photos that contained unexplained white misty areas. These photographic anomalies were all on the main stairs, an area which is the location where disembodied footsteps have been heard.

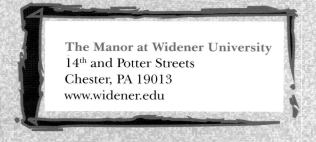

The Manor at Widener University
14th and Potter Streets
Chester, PA 19013
www.widener.edu

The Castle

Right across the street from the Manor is a large, Gothic-looking structure known as The Castle. This mansion, built in 1884, is now the home of the Delta Phi Epsilon sorority. It was originally the home of the Richard Wetherill family. He and his brother, Robert, were big in the local and world iron and steel industry. If you drive down Providence Road from The Castle towards Wallingford, you will see a huge stone mansion very similar to Richard Wetherill's Castle at 20th Street. The similarity is not coincidental. This was the home of Richard's senior brother and partner, Robert. The similarity doesn't end at the outside. Both Gothic fortresses are said to be haunted! Although the details of whom or what haunts the halls of Greystone, as Robert's castle was called, are sketchy, there are very specific accounts of who haunts The Castle at Widener.

It may be that haunted sorority houses sound like something out of a movie, but I have been assured by residents and university staff that The Castle is most definitely haunted. One staff member, who requested that I withhold his name, actually saw the Castle's ghost. He is no longer employed by Widener, but he became visibly chilled as he recounted his experiences at the Castle.

The first time he saw the ghost he thought it was a real person. He had been called to the mansion to check the fire panel in the basement. As he was working, he began to get the sensation of being watched. He turned and saw a little girl standing there by the bricked-up entrance to the tunnel that once connected the basement to a carriage house. Surprised, he asked her what she was doing there. As the words left his lips, she turned and disappeared right into the wall where the tunnel used to be.

Although he didn't feel threatened by her, he admitted that the sight of the little girl was always a little creepy. He saw her many more times after that; always in the basement, hanging around near the bricked-up tunnel entrance. There were constant problems with the heat in that place. The residents complained about frigidly cold areas and checking the heater became a regular occurrence. It got so that as he went down the stairs he would call out, "Hello!" to the little girl to try and put her at ease. He felt that there was something sad and shy about her. The last time he saw her was during his last week of work, so as far as he knows, she is still there.

As I looked up into the eyes of the former staff member, I could see that The Castle is not the only place haunted by that little girl. His mind was also haunted by images of her. He never found out who she may have been or found a name for her. He had asked around campus and the story was that she had lived there and died very young.

As I left the interview, I found myself haunted by her as well, and drove right over to the University to see what I could see. The Castle and the Manor were as beautiful as ever, but there was no sign of a ghost of a little girl or anyone else as classes were on recess for the summer. I would have to try and find her story elsewhere.

There is no record of a Wetherill child's death in the census records or family trees.

The Wetherill mausoleum at Chester Rural Cemetery has no children buried there. All family members there match with the census records. Perhaps the little girl belonged to one of the servants or she could date from a time before the house was built in 1884.

The Castle at Widener University
14th and Potter Streets
Chester, PA 19013

Who is the little girl who plays in the Castle basement?

Fickes Hall

Chatham is another college that has a large number of converted mansions. I spent a semester at Chatham and was assigned to Fickes Hall, one of the converted mansions. We got a roomy triple with a private bathroom, a fireplace, a huge walk-in closet, and a window seat that overlooked the back entrance to the dorm. It was like living in a castle.

As incoming freshmen, we were treated to a bunch of stories about old Mrs. Fickes roaming the halls at night, waiting to grab an unsuspecting girl as she walked back from the bathrooms or a late night study session. The stories were so unrealistic they bordered on the ludicrous, so I laughed them off, having grown up in a real haunted house with real ghosts.

Ouija Fun

I had brought my Ouija® board with me, but it had sat on top of the trunk at the bottom of my bed until one night when my roommates and I had some friends over. The girls from the next room came over and we sat on the beds, eating popcorn, ice cream, and swapping stories from back home. This led to some of the spooky stories from my house, which the girls loved. Every time I would finish a story, they would ask for another one. Then one of them spotted the Ouija® Board and thought it would be great to try it out.

I would love to say that things started flying off the walls and Mrs. Fickes swooped in and snatched up the planchette, but nothing happened. We got bored with it and the group broke up to go to bed.

Up to that night we had experienced nothing that would have caused me to think that our dorm was haunted. I am not sure whether it was just a coincidence, or maybe we piqued the interest of someone with our attempt at communication, but from that night on, unexplained events became a part of our daily lives.

That night we were awakened by knocking at the door. We all woke up, thinking some emergency had occurred, but when we opened the door, we were looking at an empty and dark hallway. We assumed it was our neighbors playing a joke on us until it happened again the next night, and the next, and the next. We got together and asked our friends next door to please stop the knocking as we needed some sleep and their response chilled me. They had been experiencing the same thing, only they had assumed it was us!

That night we all gathered in my dorm room again to try and see if anything would happen. One of us suggested trying the Ouija Board ® again and we did. It was a completely different experience from the one we had last time. A name was spelled out over and over again. Responses of yes and no gave us a little more information.

A Strange Visitor

The name spelled out was her name and she was a 12-year-old girl who had died there. She did not go to school there but she liked our room. She lived on the first floor. Although I am sure that readers will want to know her name, as has everyone I have told this story to, but I cannot and will not divulge it. Why? Since that night, every time this name has come up, it seemed to call the influence of this particular spirit back into my life.

We sat on the beds after the session was finished and wondered what to do next. Should we research the history? Should we pray for her? Should we try to make her leave? I asked, out loud, "What do you want us to do?" I had asked her specifically, by using her name. As I said this, a floor lamp that stood between our beds began to shake violently. I think we all held our breaths while we waited for it to stop. We tried to recreate the effect by moving around, jumping on the beds, everything we could think of! The only thing that caused the same effect was if we actually grabbed the lamp and shook it. Our friends went back to their room and thankfully, the rest of the night was uneventful.

We thought that was the end of things until we began to be accused of having guys in our room after curfew. Our neighbors on the other side of our bathroom were seniors. They complained to us that they heard men's voices in the bathroom. We assured them that we had no one in there, but they didn't believe us and reported us to the resident assistant. Now, I wish they had tried to record it!

We were called to the Dean's office to answer the charges against us. After some serious warnings from her, since they really had no evidence, we were allowed to go back to our rooms, with the knowledge that we were being watched.

More Bad "Luck"?

Things got even stranger after that. First, the girls in the room on the other side, the ones who had participated in the Ouija® session, stopped talking to us. Our third roommate suddenly turned nasty on us, filed a complaint against us, which landed us back in the Dean's office, and she ended up moving out. Our phone hardly ever worked. Most of the time we would pick it up and hear a hollow sound, like someone was listening from another extension. We asked around and had maintenance check on it but no one else was experiencing that and maintenance could find nothing wrong. They put in a new phone jack for us. That fixed things for a couple days and then it started again.

One night I was sitting in the window seat talking on the phone, which for once was not giving us a problem. Our window there overlooked the back door. I heard a noise from outside so I looked down and saw a girl by the back door. She motioned for me to come down. This was very common for us. The front door was locked at 11 p.m. and after that time we had to use our key to get in the back door. If we forgot the key, we had to ring for the Resident Assistant to open the door. Most of us didn't like to wake up the RA, so if there was a light on in the window of our room, girls would often throw a rock to get one of us to let her in.

So, I waved back and went down to open the door. When I got there, I didn't see anyone. I looked out and saw the back of the girl as she was heading towards the front door. "Hey!" I yelled after her. She didn't stop. I took off one of my shoes and stuck it in the door to keep it open and started walking towards her. "Hey!" I yelled again, "The door is…" my voice died as she turned to face me. Her face was unnaturally pale and something about her eyes absolutely chilled me. I did not recognize her and there was something evil and inhuman about her.

I turned to run back to the propped door, and to my horror, the door was now closed and my shoe was outside. I looked behind me to see where she was. The scariest part of all this was while I was banging on the door and yelling, she was walking so slowly, as if she knew she had plenty of time to catch up with me. I had about five seconds to decide what to do or I would be trapped.

I took off running around the other side of the building, away from her, taking the long way around to the front door. I threw myself toward the door, ringing the bell frantically. The RA opened the door and I almost ran her over getting in. She started walking towards the phone, probably to call campus security, and I said, "No, please don't."

"What is going on?" she asked, concerned.

I told her that I thought someone was following me, but I didn't want her to call security. She looked at me curiously and invited me to sit for a minute. She stood, looking expectantly, and I told her I thought I saw a ghost. She looked back at me oddly and then told me to just go to bed. I did make her go with me to get my shoe.

I got back up to my room and saw that my roommate was still out. I went over to the phone to see if my friend was still hanging on, but there was no sound at all. I hung it up and looked out the window.

She was back, standing out there, staring up at the window. I decided to call one of my other friends in the dorm and sleep in her room that night. I never saw her again after that. I never found out who she was or what she was. I became very ill shortly after that and had to leave school.

To this day, I will not speak the name that was given to us on the Ouija ® Board. A few of the things that happened when the name was mentioned include:

- My microwave door shattered because somehow a small straight pin ended up inside.
- A serious car accident occurred that totaled my car.
- A glass exploded in my and a friend's face as it flew out of a cabinet.
- I fell all the way down a flight of steps in my home and was seriously injured when I tripped over a mysteriously torn piece of carpet.

I have not heard of any subsequent incidents similar to the ones I experienced at Chatham. I concluded that it was a combination of the right person (me) in the right place (haunted dorm) that combined to awaken something that was probably there all along and just waiting for the key that fit the lock to set it free. I don't know if she is still around. I have not spoken her name in about ten years.

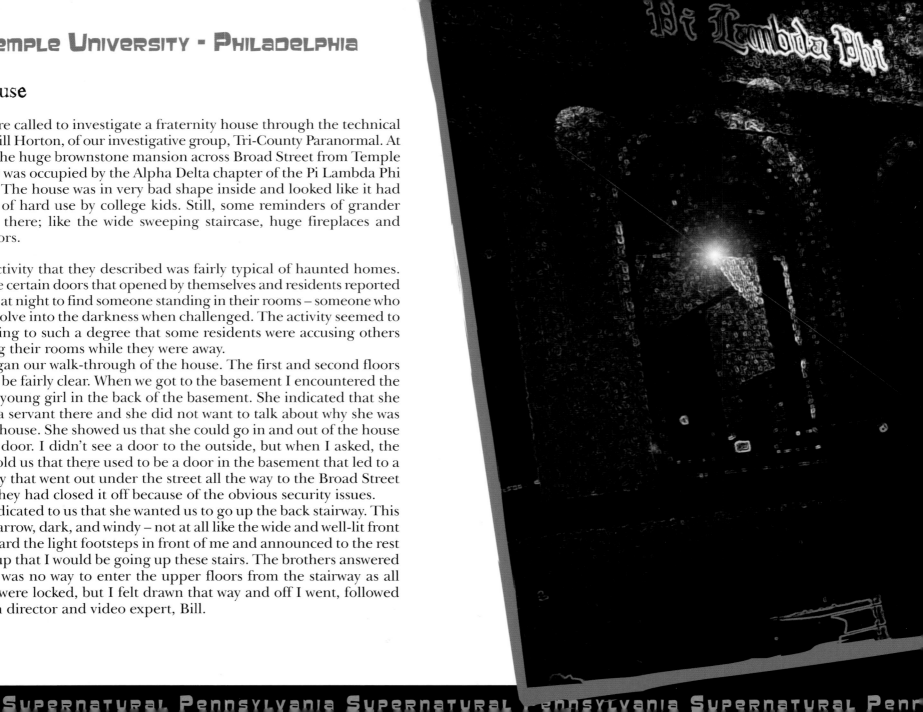

Temple University - Philadelphia

Frat House

We were called to investigate a fraternity house through the technical director, Bill Horton, of our investigative group, Tri-County Paranormal. At the time, the huge brownstone mansion across Broad Street from Temple University was occupied by the Alpha Delta chapter of the Pi Lambda Phi fraternity. The house was in very bad shape inside and looked like it had seen a lot of hard use by college kids. Still, some reminders of grander days were there; like the wide sweeping staircase, huge fireplaces and pocket doors.

The activity that they described was fairly typical of haunted homes. There were certain doors that opened by themselves and residents reported waking up at night to find someone standing in their rooms – someone who would dissolve into the darkness when challenged. The activity seemed to be increasing to such a degree that some residents were accusing others of entering their rooms while they were away.

We began our walk-through of the house. The first and second floors seemed to be fairly clear. When we got to the basement I encountered the ghost of a young girl in the back of the basement. She indicated that she had been a servant there and she did not want to talk about why she was still at the house. She showed us that she could go in and out of the house through a door. I didn't see a door to the outside, but when I asked, the brothers told us that there used to be a door in the basement that led to a passageway that went out under the street all the way to the Broad Street Subway. They had closed it off because of the obvious security issues.

She indicated to us that she wanted us to go up the back stairway. This was very narrow, dark, and windy – not at all like the wide and well-lit front stairs. I heard the light footsteps in front of me and announced to the rest of the group that I would be going up these stairs. The brothers answered that there was no way to enter the upper floors from the stairway as all the doors were locked, but I felt drawn that way and off I went, followed by my tech director and video expert, Bill.

The once-grand entry hall of the beautiful
Philadelphia brownstone.
Photo courtesy of Bill Horton.

When we got to the top of the stairs, there was a doorway and a very small landing. I felt like I had stepped into a cold spot and asked to Bill, "Do you feel that?" He responded that he could feel something on the hair on his knuckles. When we reviewed the recording, right after he says that, there was a small, whispery voice that sounds as if it was almost giggling. It said, "Hairy knuckles, hairy knuckles!" It remains one of my favorite recordings we have from haunted locations.

We entered the room and went from that room through to the next. A short time later the rest of the group came up the front stairs and wanted to know how we got in there. We told him we had just walked in and he could not believe that door was open, because that room was the one where most of the problems had been experienced, leading the occupant to be extremely vigilant about locking the doors. Not only that, he said he would have no reason to have the back door unlocked, as they did not use that stairway.

The last thing that night that I picked up on was that the girl seemed very disturbed by the renovations that had been done. In particular, she seemed confused by the lighting fixtures and she was showing me the that lights used to be up, but now they are down. I asked the brothers about this. They looked at each other and then said, "That is so funny. When the lights were put in, they were accidentally placed upside down. They should be up." When we left for the night we made arrangements to return and try to help the resident spirit find peace, or at least try to convince her to stop leaving doors unlocked.

The seance was held in one of the most active rooms of the house. We quickly made contact with the spirit of the young girl who called herself "Ammie." My conclusion was that this may have been short for Amelia or perhaps she was speaking with an accent and I was misunderstanding the pronunciation.

She agreed to cross over to the spirit world and asked if "the others" could come with her. I told her that all spirits were welcome in the light and suddenly a very strong, cold wind whooshed through the room and I saw a large number of spirits crossing through. I wondered where they were all coming from and the answer came through loudly and clearly, "They are from the funeral home." There was a funeral home three houses down from the fraternity house, called Morris Rosenberg's Son, Inc. As quick as the wind blew up, it ended and everything seemed very peaceful again.

About a year later, I was driving by the University and glanced over at the fraternity house. To my dismay I saw that there was a big lock on the door and the house appeared to be abandoned.

I thought about the house from time to time and played the "Hairy Knuckles" recording at lectures and wondered if there were new residents. This year I was contacted by the *University Newspaper* because they were writing a piece on haunted places at Temple. I told her that as far as we knew, it was no longer haunted because the spirits had all left. They wanted to include the story of the investigation anyway and they told me that there was a new fraternity occupying the house this year. So far, they had encountered no ghosts.

Spooky Stories and Legends

We all know them and tell them around campfires and at slumber parties. They are part of American folklore—urban legends, that always contain a grain of truth somewhere, if you dig deep enough. Some of these famous spooky stories have their origins in Pennsylvania.

I was 12 years old and standing in a dark bathroom in front of the sink with my eyes closed. My friends stood on guard outside the door, waiting. I tried to keep my voice steady as I recited, "Mary Worth, I love you" ten times in a row. Then I yelled out, "Mary Worth I hate you!" I opened my eyes and saw blackness in front of me.

"Where is my face?" I wondered. It should have been reflected in the mirror in front of me..." Oh! There, "I whispered as my eyes adjusted to the darkness and I began to make out the pale outline in the mirror.

"What's happening?" My friends whispered through the door.

"Nothing," I replied and then leaned forward. Was there something moving in the darkness behind me? In a panic, I turned and threw the door open, sighing in relief as I slammed the door behind me.

My friends all looked at me expectantly. They wanted to know what happened. Not wanting to disappoint them, I described the red eyes, long fingernails and scraggly hair on a figure that emerged from the darkness behind me. I even thought she may have touched my shoulder! My shoulder was examined for signs of fingernail marks, which we all swore we saw forming on the skin there.

My experience with the legend of Bloody Mary has probably been repeated in dark bathrooms at 6th grade slumber parties all over the United States. The girls all tell their own version of what they see or think they see in the mirror. No one wants to admit they got scared of the dark bathroom mirror, so they talk about the witch who emerged to attack them.

My daughter told me that she had also gone into a dark bathroom, stood in front of a mirror and said, "Bloody Mary" three times before she got scared and ran out. What scared her?

She doesn't know. She was afraid of what might happen. She had heard that as long as you didn't actually see Bloody Mary, you would be okay. If you did see her, she would follow you for the rest of your life, waiting in the dark to kill you with her axe.

The Real Mary?

Some say that every legend contains a grain of truth. When I started researching haunted places in Pennsylvania, I thought I may have actually found the original Bloody Mary in Pennsylvania! Her name was Mary Johnson Black and it is said she was a witch. She's buried in the Tindall family cemetery in Shenango Township, Lawrence County.

Her grave can be located after following the path from the road until you arrive at the swamp, go around the swamp on the left side. Her grave is separate from the others and is unmarked.

She must have been a child prodigy because research revealed that she was born in 1801 and died in 1888. According to an entry from S. Slater on ancestry.com, many of the grave markers in the Tindall cemetery have been destroyed or stolen, possibly due to this legend of Bloody Mary. Mary Black's tombstone was found in the swamp and is now kept at the Lawrence County Historical Society, where it is kept safe from further abuse.

Kathy's first experience with the paranormal happened when she was about 7 years old. She had chicken pox and so did a couple of the children of friends of her family. The infected children were staying together at her house. As they were getting ready for bed one night, they saw a bright light shining through her bedroom window. She had a hard time describing the brightness; she just described it as very, very bright. They wanted to see what it was, so she and her friend jumped up and ran to the window. They looked out and incredibly, across the road in a meadow, there was a large sailing ship that looked like it was sinking! It was surrounded by a brilliant halo of light and it was glowing. She vividly remembered looking at her friend's spotty face as she looked back at her and they ran over to Kathy's parents' room. Her parents were seeing it too! They were standing at their window looking at the big ship in the meadow. Not long after that it faded out and disappeared. Her parents looked like they were in shock, and Kathy's mother walked them back to the bedroom to put them to bed. She is about 50 years old now, but claims that she will never forget how bright the glow of that ship was.

I had a lot of questions when she first told me the story. My first thought was, "UFO enthusiasts would say this was a UFO." It didn't sound like any UFO sighting I have ever heard, so I did some research. The experience that Kathy and her family had could be explained in two different ways; one paranormal, one natural.

Ship o' the Dead or Mirage?

The paranormal explanation that I found was that of the legendary Ship o' the Dead. This legend holds that "when an old and retired sailor dies, a ghostly ship comes to take his spirit away. This is especially true if the sailor had been a pirate. The ship will appear wherever he is, even over land, in which case it will sail through the air."

The other explanation is more mundane, but still very intriguing. Could this have been some sort of mirage? Throughout history there have been accounts of phantom armies and cities appearing in the sky.

A mirage is generated when two layers of air at different temperatures come into contact. Since cold air is denser than hot air, the boundary between the layers can refract, or bend, light. This effect is especially noticeable if the light hits the boundary at an extreme angle. The classic "oasis in the desert" mirage occurs when the air just above the ground gets hot when the ground heats it.

When I visited Scotland, I heard stories of phantom armies. The Lord of Kingswells and his companion reported witnessing an army of at least 7,000 soldiers. It was early in the morning, and a clear sunny day. What they saw was so real that they could make out the battalion's colors, see the drums carried by the drummers and that the commanding officer was riding a white horse. The two men watched the army for two hours until it eventually disappeared behind a hill.

The same army, led by the same commander was seen later the same year. On that occasion, it was said that the witnesses could see smoke coming from the muskets but they heard no sound of shots fired. Another phantom army appeared floating above a mountain in Scotland. This was witnessed by a solitary man. Like the other sightings, the apparition lasted for a couple of hours until the army disappeared behind a hill once again.

There are consistencies in the eye-witness accounts of the phantom army sightings. All appear in great detail; enough to make witnesses think they are seeing a real army, but in all cases the armies are silent. The duration of the sightings are always of a sustained period of time and occur during good visibility, clear skies and sunshine.

I was unable to find any account of a phantom ship appearing over land, other than the old legend related above. Phantom ships are often reported at sea, and are said to be a reflection or a trick of the light that makes an actual far-off vessel appear to be floating in the sky. "So why are these vessels always old-fashioned ones?" I wondered. Well, there is no explanation for that.

What did this family see when they looked out the windows and observed this glowing ship in the sky? Was it a mirage or a trick of the light? I am not completely convinced that it was either. The witnesses claimed no connection to ships or pirates and seemed to be completely confounded as to why a ship would appear floating over a meadow in Frazer, Pennsylvania.

Perhaps at that moment in 1964 in Frazer, an old sailor passed away and this group of people was lucky enough to have been in the right place at the right time to witness the legendary the ship o' the dead as it came to take him away...

The Windigo

Winters in Pennsylvania, especially western Pennsylvania, can be harsh. Snow piles up and the wind chill makes it dangerously cold. When I was a young child in Washington, Pennsylvania, I heard stories every winter about the Windigo.

"Be careful or the Windigo will get you!" the older kids would tell us when we played in the woods behind our homes.

"The Windigo will get you and take you away and eat you!"

My mother assured me that the Windigo was just a legend, but when I was outside, alone on the snowy paths to my friends' houses I wasn't too sure. So many times I swore I heard the heavy footsteps of the Windigo in the brush off the path.

The Windigo was described to us as a huge, hairy beast who lurked in the winter woods, looking for people to capture and eat. It had been around in these woods as long as anyone could remember. The Native American legends talked about him.

We moved away to Philadelphia, and the Windigo became a distant memory to me until one Christmas when I went to visit my father in Washington where I'd grown up. We went to get something from the car one night and he called, "Be careful out there!" In an instant I was five years old again, and picturing a huge, hairy Windigo lurking in the fields across the street.

Turns out that my father was trying to warn us about coyotes in the area. He didn't even remember anything about a Windigo.

When I got home I started doing research on the Windigo and found that it was really a Native American legend. The Windigo legend varies a little from tribe to tribe, but all seem to agree that it is born of starvation. When a man is driven to consume the flesh of another human being, he will be possessed by the spirit of a Windigo. When a man becomes possessed by this spirit, he is driven by a compulsive hunger for human flesh. Over time, with every person he eats, he grows larger, uglier and hairier; becoming more animal than human.

The Windigo seems to me to be a Native American version of the European werewolf legend. Instead of the full moon, he is transformed by the season, and, like the werewolf, one can also be transformed into a Windigo by being bitten by a Windigo or by a shaman placing a curse. I could not find any "cures" for being a Windigo, but a Windigo can be killed by burning the body of its host and scattering the ashes.

I was surprised to find that the Windigo does not just live in legend. There is a Windigo Isle Royale National Park in Michigan and a disorder known as "Windigo Psychosis," which is characterized by a desire to eat the flesh of humans.

Pennsylvania's Spookiest, Creepiest Places

If you think the preceding stories and places were too spooky or creepy, then read no further, because we have saved the spookiest and creepiest places in Pennsylvania for last.

Some of these places are where you would expect to find creepy and spooky stories; on battlefields, in decaying prisons, and in old colonial-era inns. The others are where you least expect them to be, in our homes, behind bedrooms doors, and lurking in kitchens and attics.

Please be aware before reading this section; during the writing of these entries I experienced a great deal of paranormal activity in my home.

The Spookiest House - Ridley Township

Nearly every time I present a lecture about ghosts and hauntings I am asked, "What is the scariest place you have ever been in?" I answer without hesitation, "My grandmother's house." My grandmother's house is where I had my first encounter with the paranormal and it is the only place I would not want to go back to. It is still a private home, so unfortunately I cannot divulge the exact location. When my grandmother died we were all offered a chance to buy the house. Not one person in my family wanted it, even though it is in a prime location. I think we all had our experiences there.

When I was very young, we lived in western Pennsylvania. My mother was from Delaware County, Pennsylvania, and my father was from Western Pennsylvania. We came back east to visit my mother's family from time to time. On this particular visit, I was about four years old and my sister was about two. We were sleeping in my mother's childhood bedroom, all in the same double bed. My sister woke up screaming in the middle of the night. She was pointing to the area between the bedroom door and the wall. My mother had left the bedroom door slightly ajar to let in light from the hallway. "Monster!" she screamed, "Frankenstein!"

My mother began to gather her up to take her out of the room. I peered into the darkness towards the area and I saw it. There

was a huge shadowy outline of a person there. The vibe it was giving off was very menacing. As I lay there, immobilized with fear, my mother left the room and shut the door. She didn't realize I was also awake.

The shadow began moving towards me and I did the thing that comes natural to a four-year old. I pulled the covers up over my head and shut my eyes tightly. After what seemed like forever I peeked out and the shadow was still there, right next to the bed and it seemed to be looking at me with interest. I pulled the covers back up and spent the rest of the night like that. When I asked about it the next morning, I was told that it was all a nightmare.

That was a typical answer from my grandmother when she was asked about the things that happened in that house. It was our imagination, a nightmare, too many cookies, or it was a squirrel in the attic. Even things that happened right in front of groups of us were dismissed. When I got older, I realized it may have been a self-preservation attempt on the part of my grandmother. She had to live there with whatever unseen entities lurked in the rooms of the old house.

I didn't technically live there, but every day after school we would walk to my grandmother's and we would be there until after dinner, when she would take us back to our house. This was our normal daily routine.

Summers and school holidays would mean we would be there all day. If we were sick, we stayed with Mom-mom in her haunted house.

Footsteps across the upstairs floor were a regular occurrence. There was one door in particular that would not stay closed. This room, which we called the green room because it had green wallpaper, had been my mother's room when she lived there. There was a small doorway that went to the attic under the eaves of the roof. This doorway had a very scary, negative feeling to it. When I stayed there I always pushed the dresser in front of it. This door seemed to be the doorway, or portal to all the negative energy in the house. Many times I woke up in the middle of the night, aware of a presence emerging from that doorway. As I got older it was clear that the presence in the bedroom was female.

She appeared to be a large-boned, heavy-set woman with hard eyes and a stiff mouth. She glared at me from the corners of the room and from behind the door that never wanted to stay shut. No wonder my sister had called her a "Frankenstein monster." She would just stare at me, never speaking, and after a while she would go back into the attic door.

The basement was another matter altogether. If the weather was bad, my sister and I

The basement corner
where the ghost lives.

were sent down to the basement to play. It was a nice, big open space; perfect for roller skating. We should have been happy down there, but we were never comfortable. There was one corner of the basement, back by the heater where the floor was sunk in a rectangular shape about six feet long by two and a half feet wide. It so closely resembled a grave to us that we always referred to that corner as "where the ghost was buried."

As I got older, I spent more and more time at my grandmother's house. Sometimes my friends would come by after school or in the evenings to hang out. My best friend and I would wait to see if the ghost would make her presence known. One night was particularly memorable. We were sitting at the kitchen table talking to two male friends. When the subject of our ghosts came up, one of the boys was very dismissive of it and claimed that he did not believe in ghosts. When we persisted with our stories of footsteps, doors opening, and the presence upstairs and in the basement, he announced to the room, "If there is a ghost here then they better do something now!"

A few seconds of silence passed and the cookie tin that was on the table suddenly slid across the table, gaining momentum, and then flew off the table and against the wall before falling to the floor. We all got up and walked out the door and down the driveway, glancing behind us every few steps.

"What the heck was that?" he asked when we got to the side-walk.

"That was the ghost!" my girl friend and I replied. We had long ago accepted that these kind of things were a normal occurrence at the house.

We stood outside, staring at the front of the house. It was so odd that we felt more comfortable outside in the dark than inside the house. The boys that hung out with us that night came back to the house once more after that. The one who had challenged the ghost wouldn't stay inside. When we asked him what was wrong, he replied that as soon as he walked in the door he felt like someone wanted to kill him. He never set foot in the house again, preferring to wait outside in all kinds of rain and snow rather than wait inside for us.

I began asking other family members if they had experienced anything unusual at my grandmother's house. She continued to deny that there was anything paranormal going on there, but I simply had no other explanation for some of the things I had witnessed.

My mother, whose old bedroom was the green room, told me right away that she was always uncomfortable in that room and felt as if there was "something evil" in the attic that was waiting for the chance to come out and get her. My cousin who had stayed in that room said the same thing. She said that when she stayed there she would move the chest of drawers over in front of the door.

Things continued in the house pretty much on the same level until my grandmother became very ill. The decision was made to put her on hospice and we took turns caring for her around the clock. It was almost as if the house knew she was dying. Unexplained footsteps and scratching in the walls was an almost constant occurrence. Lights turned on and off of their own accord and one lamp in the kitchen would periodically turn on even when it was unplugged.

After her death, when we were clearing out the house, the presences there continued to make sure we knew they were there. I wondered what was going to happen when the house was sold. Realtors who showed the house for us came back and asked us if it was haunted. None of us would be alone there.

After one visit, my youngest daughter, who was five years old at the time, asked us what was going to happen to the man in the basement. I tried to respond in an even voice, even though I was completely shocked by this question.

"What man?" I asked her.

"The man from the basement. He tried to help Mom-mom, but she was too sick. He's sad," she replied.

"What did he look like?"

"He was dark brown."

"Did he tell you his name?"

"Yes, Cocojam."

"Cocojam?" I questioned. I wanted to make sure the name was correct.

"Yeah," she said. During the rest of the conversation she revealed more of the story. From her description, we concluded that she was describing an African-American man. She claimed that he told her he died there and he was trying to take care of my grandmother. When we asked her how he had died, she thought for a minute and said, "He holded a gun the wrong way and then he died."

My mother and I both got chills. We had discussed the feelings of being watched while we were in the basement and our feeling that there was something funny about that sunken area in the floor. Our research into the history of the house had not turned up much, but there were some clues. It had been a farm at one time because the building that we used as a garage was definitely a converted barn, complete with a bunk room, hayloft, and the remains of horses' stalls.

The Delaware County records have the date of the house's construction as 1900. The 1900 map shows one house and barn in the area. The land, house, and barn were owned by Jesse W. Johnson. He was 69 years old in 1900 and he lived there with his widowed sister and

This attic door was the source of negative energy.

her two sons. No occupation is listed for Jesse. The 1909 map still has the property listed under his name and shows the house and barn. One of his nephews was a lawyer and the other was a grocery clerk. Jesse does not appear in the 1910 census, so it is likely that he passed away. Johnson is still listed as the owner of the property where our house was in 1932, but the parcel is much smaller and subdivided.

Sometimes I think we will never find out who or what haunts that house. Once in a while I drive by if I am in the neighborhood, but it always gives me that uncomfortable feeling of being watched. Whatever spirit inhabits that house knows that I am driving by at that moment – I am sure of it. Even now, as I think about the house and the time I spent there, I can feel it reaching out and touching the edges of my mind, like fingers probing for an opening or a door in a dark room. Although I have moved away and it has been more than five years since I have been in that house, it haunts me still.

Gettysburg Battlefield - Gettysburg

This three-day battle in July of 1863 was the bloodiest battle of the Civil War. A little over ten percent of the men who fought there lost their lives on the battlefield and more died shortly after of their injuries. It was a pivotal battle that turned the tide of the war for the Confederacy.

When the Confederate army left Gettysburg, the fields and roads were still strewn with the bodies of fallen soldiers. Most homes and businesses were serving as hospitals. Today many of them proudly show off blood-stained floors from that summer. It seems not supernatural, but natural that such a place would be haunted.

The fighting was not just in the battlefield park. Skirmishes occurred all along the roads leading in and out of Gettysburg. There was fighting in the streets and through the farm fields. My most interesting experiences occurred in The Comfort Inn on Route 30, in the basement of the Soldier's Museum, and at Devil's Den, near the Sniper's Hole. I even had the ghost of a Confederate soldier follow me home because I reminded him of his sister!

The most compelling experience I had on Gettysburg Battlefield occurred in the slaughter pen, which is in the forest across from Devil's Den. The area was full of ghost hunters from a ghost conference. I walked off by myself, into the woods, and I heard footsteps off to my right. I didn't think anything of it, and continued with my recording, asking questions like, "Is anyone here?" I took a few pictures, and as I snapped the last one, I noticed someone in front of me. I began to apologize for temporarily blinding this person, when I realized who, or what it was.

He was staring straight ahead, off to my left and he was walking with a purpose. He had on dark clothing and a dark cap. He walked right on by like I was not even there; he never even changed the rhythm of his step. Then he disappeared, and it felt like time started again.

I have traveled to Gettysburg so many times in the hopes of capturing some evidence or experiencing something supernatural. This experience was strange to me, because I should have been thrilled but I was not. During that experience and when I reflect on it, I feel the same sadness and hopelessness. After I saw him that night, I lost all interest in further investigation and wanted to go back to my hotel.

Did I pick up on the feelings of a long-dead soldier? I felt so sad for that man, lost in time and space, compelled to attempt and re-attempt to complete a mission he will never complete. If I ever do see him again, maybe I can get some answers. Until that time, or the end of time, I pray for his soul's peace.

This was what appeared in the photo taken of the pale Union soldier.

A ghostly mist swirls on the battlefield.
Photo courtesy of Rich Hickman.

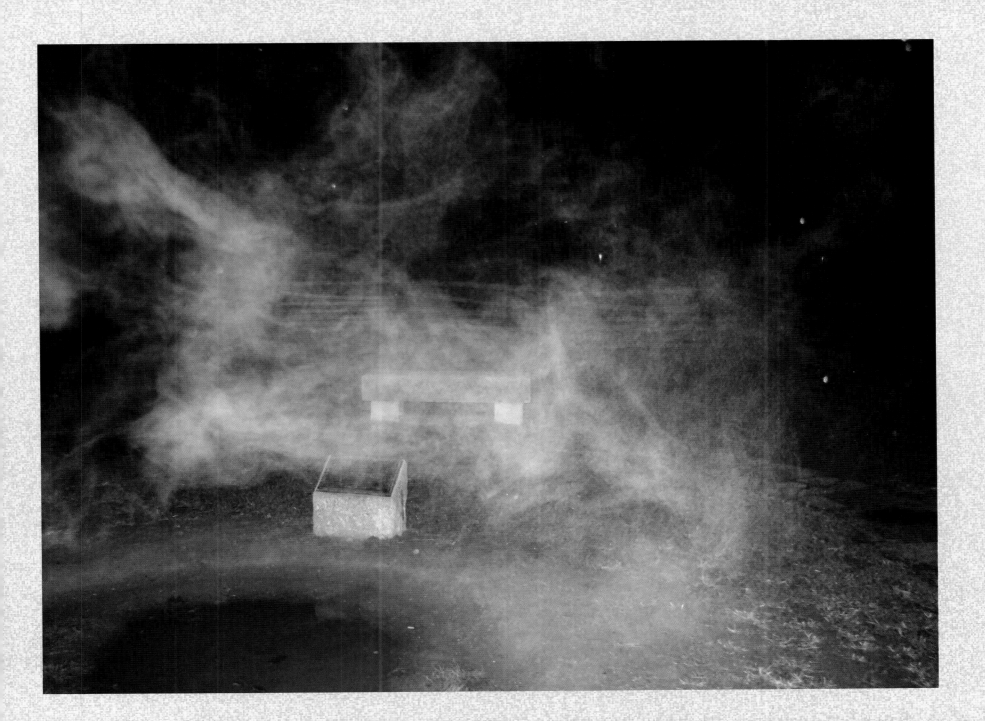

The Jennie Wade House - Gettysburg

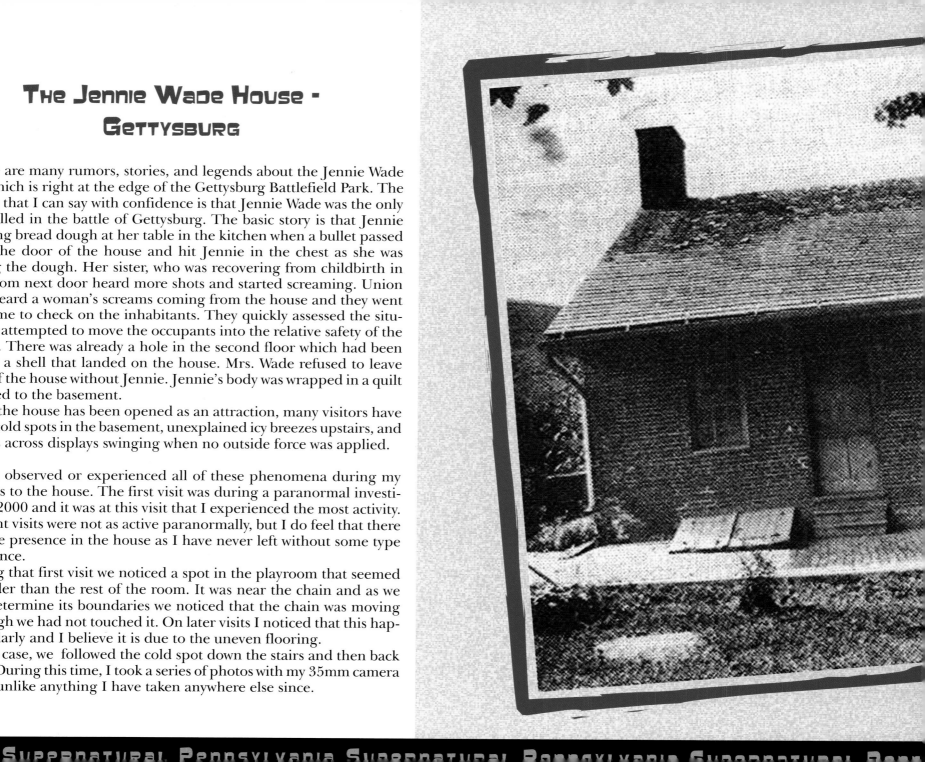

There are many rumors, stories, and legends about the Jennie Wade House, which is right at the edge of the Gettysburg Battlefield Park. The one thing that I can say with confidence is that Jennie Wade was the only civilian killed in the battle of Gettysburg. The basic story is that Jennie was making bread dough at her table in the kitchen when a bullet passed through the door of the house and hit Jennie in the chest as she was preparing the dough. Her sister, who was recovering from childbirth in the bedroom next door heard more shots and started screaming. Union soldiers heard a woman's screams coming from the house and they went to the home to check on the inhabitants. They quickly assessed the situation and attempted to move the occupants into the relative safety of the basement. There was already a hole in the second floor which had been caused by a shell that landed on the house. Mrs. Wade refused to leave her side of the house without Jennie. Jennie's body was wrapped in a quilt and carried to the basement.

Since the house has been opened as an attraction, many visitors have reported cold spots in the basement, unexplained icy breezes upstairs, and the chains across displays swinging when no outside force was applied.

I have observed or experienced all of these phenomena during my many visits to the house. The first visit was during a paranormal investigation in 2000 and it was at this visit that I experienced the most activity. Subsequent visits were not as active paranormally, but I do feel that there is an active presence in the house as I have never left without some type of experience.

During that first visit we noticed a spot in the playroom that seemed much colder than the rest of the room. It was near the chain and as we tried to determine its boundaries we noticed that the chain was moving even though we had not touched it. On later visits I noticed that this happens regularly and I believe it is due to the uneven flooring.

In any case, we followed the cold spot down the stairs and then back up again. During this time, I took a series of photos with my 35mm camera that were unlike anything I have taken anywhere else since.

Mist forming in the children's room.

I have never gotten one EVP at this site, so I have no tangible clues as to the identity of this spirit. In *Ghosts of Gettysburg IV*, by Mark Nesbitt, it says that one of the spirits in the basement is the spirit of Jennie's father, but that there are other spirits present. I have not seen any evidence that would identify the spirit or spirits as any particular person; however, on my last visit there I received an insight about the Jennie Wade house that may provide an answer.

For some reason, there are many sites in Gettysburg that would like to be the place where Jennie Wade was shot from. My insight related to the shooting and I believe where the fatal shot was fired from was somewhere near the road and not from inside any house on that street.

As I sat in the basement of the Jennie Wade house, I became aware of the ghostly presence of a Union soldier. I asked him what he was doing there and he told me that he wanted to take responsibility for what he did. He said he was one of the soldiers that helped carry Jennie Wade's body to the basement. He and another soldier were looking for some Confederate soldiers they had seen running in the direction of the Farnsworth House.

Misty shape on the stairs as I followed a cold spot.

As they looked across at the house and up towards the hill past the Wade House, they saw the enemy soldiers running up near the hillside, so they began firing. To his horror he heard a woman start screaming from the house. They ran as quickly as they could toward the house to offer help, but as they came in the door they saw that Jennie Wade was dead. He knew he had shot her accidentally, and he was consumed with guilt. He and his companion promised to keep the rest of the family safe. When he saw how devastated her mother was, his heart broke and he felt like he did not deserve to live himself. He said that he was killed later in the battle, but he returned there to watch over the family and try to keep them safe. The worst thing was when he realized that others were blamed for what he had done. Although it did seem difficult for him to tell this whole story and I am not sure if it could ever be proven or disproven, that was the story he told me. I made sure to tell him that he did not have to stay there, but he indicated that he still felt obligated to watch over the people there.

The basement of this house is a place that many, many people have sent me unusual photos from along with their encounters with the ghosts there. The other actively haunted areas are the playroom, the upstairs bedroom on the basement side, and the two stairways.

Jenny Wade House
548 Baltimore Street
Gettysburg, PA 17325
(717) 334-4100

Another mist forms on the other staircase.

Eastern State Penitentiary - Philadelphia

This place is one that is actively haunted day and night and I can say that I have had an experience every time I was there. Every area of this prison museum seems to have some kind of activity, but the areas that we have experienced the most activity are Death Row, Cell Block 12, and the workshop area.

One night during an investigation there, every time I would walk out of Death Row, we heard banging coming from the second floor. There was no one up there as the second floor was not accessible at the time. When I came back in, the banging would stop. We weren't sure what was causing it, but it sounded eerily like a person banging on the metal cell door.

The activity on Cell Block 12 seemed to be concentrated on the second tier. As I and another investigator walked the block, trying to get a feel for where the best place to set up was, we actually heard a voice come from one of the empty cells. When we reviewed the recording, we heard it as well. It was a man's voice that said, "You don't scare me."

On another visit to the prison museum, I was standing against the rail at the top tier with my hands resting on it and I felt a large hand close over my right hand. The oddest thing about it was that the hand did not feel cold, as one would expect from a ghostly grip. It was warm and slightly clammy, as if the person was nervous or upset.

The workshop areas are outside the main prison and consist of a series of small buildings. We entered one workshop and began exploring. As I started to walk into the back workroom of this particular shop, we all heard a loud bang as if a door had closed. We walked back to see if that were the case and it wasn't, so I started walking back to the workroom again. Once more, the same thing occurred as I got about halfway in.

We decided to test it out and I backed up and tried another time. The same thing happened again. I looked around at the ground to see if I was stepping on something that could have caused it but saw nothing. Then I looked up and my breath caught in my throat. Right above me, dangling from a broken skylight was a huge, jagged piece of glass. It was moving slightly in the breeze and I backed slowly away and finally was able to breathe again. Some unseen presence was trying to keep me away from a very dangerous place. I thanked him out loud and have thanked him again on subsequent visits.

There is one other area that I feel is very haunted at Eastern State. This is the place known as the Hole. It is not accessible to the public, but you can see it through a grate. The first time I went there, I felt the energy emanating from the Hole before I got up to it. The feeling that oozes from this area is one of overwhelming doom and certain death.

The prison was built with the intention of reforming prisoners rather than just containing them. To that end, prisoners confined there experienced a solitary confinement so that they could reflect on their sins. They even spent their time outside alone as each cell had its own small, private yard. This system was eventually found to cause a great deal of mental illness among those confined there and was abandoned. The prison itself was abandoned by the state in 1971, but was never abandoned by the ghostly residents that still consider the penitentiary their home.

A phantom hand touched mine as I held the railing in Cell Block 12.

This photo of Death Row showed an unexplained shape.

Fort Mifflin - Philadelphia

If you can only visit one haunted place in Pennsylvania, make it Fort Mifflin. It is a truly amazing and historically significant place. It was at this fort that a small number of brave Patriot soldiers were able to hold off the British forces long enough for Washington and his men to escape Philadelphia. Although it was an active military base until 1954, this was the only time in the fort's history that it was actively involved in battle.

The ghosts of the fort are of soldiers, prisoners, wives, children, and even people who worked there. The exact number of ghostly inhabitants is not known and there are paranormal experiences reported in every area of the fort. Many people have photos, video, and audio recordings that support the experiences visitors have had there. Many paranormal photos and audio EVP recordings are posted online at http://www.fortmif-flinghosts.com.

The Officer's Quarters

Long known as the haunt of the Screaming Woman, this building also is the home of at least three more ghosts. There is a little girl named Katherine, a man who called himself The Colonel, and another man who seems to be on some type of guard duty. For years the screaming woman was said to be Elizabeth Pratt, an officer's wife who, devastated by her daughter's elopement with an enlisted man, committed suicide.

This story always seemed too convenient for me. Recent research has revealed that Elizabeth Pratt did not live in the Officer's Quarters and did not kill herself. Some researchers believe a different Elizabeth is the screaming woman. I am not convinced. There are very few firsthand accounts of the screaming woman, and no proof that the screams emanate from inside the fort. The officer's quarters are right next to the edge of the fort.

I have heard the screaming woman, and so has Lorraine Irby, the office manager at the fort. We both agreed that the scream sounded like a young woman being tortured to death. The marsh outside the fort has been the site of rapes and murders of young women, especially in the latter part of the twentieth century. It is possible that the screaming woman is one of these young victims.

Is the Officer's Quarters haunted by a screaming woman?

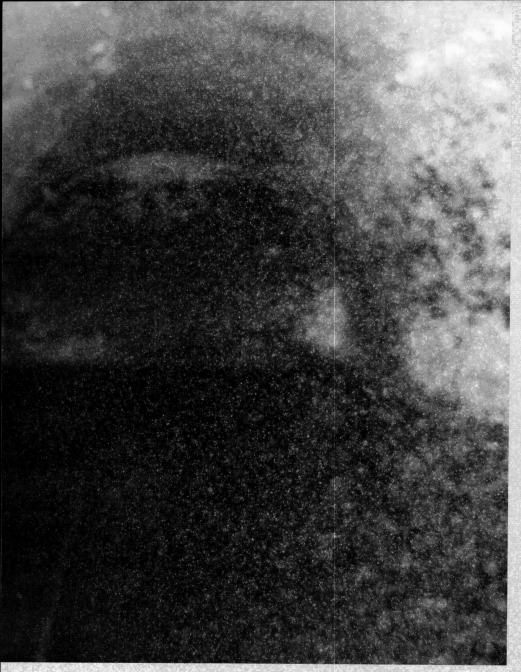

The Powder Magazine

A Revolutionary War soldier has been seen outside the entrance to this structure. Footsteps are heard in the hallway and many paranormal investigators have recorded EVPs there. My favorite EVP from the location was captured by one of our lead investigators. It is a man's voice saying, "I'm a bad boy, come play with me."

During two of our investigations on October 22, 2008, and also on February 15, 2009, a shadowy figure was seen moving quickly away from the powder magazine and up the embankment.

The Blacksmith Shop

Believed to be the oldest building at the fort, the Blacksmith Shop is said to be haunted by a blacksmith named Jacob. He wanted the doors to the shop kept open because of the heat, but the Commandant at the time wanted them kept closed. The door is said to open by itself.

Although neither I nor anyone during our events there have witnessed the door opening, I and many others have witnessed the tools that hang on the wall start to swing by themselves.

Mist seems to be forming inside the Powder Magazine.

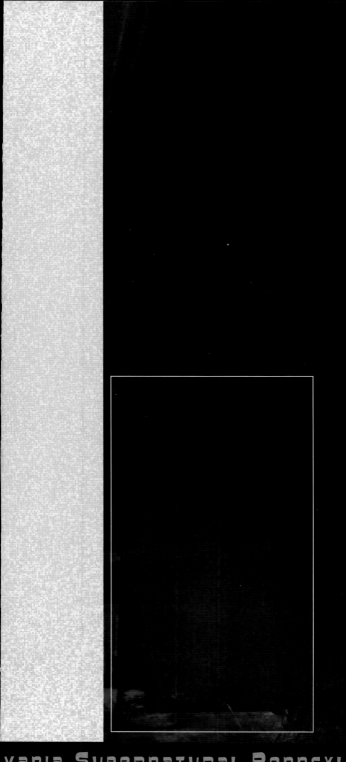

The Commandant's House

This partially restored structure is haunted by a ghost named Henry, who identified himself as a servant there. He is heard walking on the now nonexistent second floor and his voice can be heard speaking aloud to those who are willing to listen quietly and patiently. He has also been known to touch the legs of visitors, especially if the legs are bare.

The door to this house has also, on occasion, slammed shut behind someone as they exit. This happened to me one day right after a particularly noisy group of tourists had left. When I told Lorraine Irby, the office manager, about this, she said that the same thing had happened to her once. It was almost as if someone inside was saying, "Enough! Leave me alone now."

Casemates 1 – 5

A hotspot for paranormal activity, the casemates are a popular spot for investigation. They were originally constructed as a fort defense when Fort Mifflin was rebuilt after the American Revolution. Casemate 1 is the first of the casemates and is the largest. It was used as a barracks and as a prison cell for Confederate prisoners during the Civil War. Casemates 2 – 5 were also used as prison cells. Every one of these casemates has had paranormal activity, but casemates 4 and 5 have been the location of the most aggressive and violent manifestations.

The spirit that is encountered here does not like women, especially aggressive/assertive ones. On one occasion, I was knocked to the ground by an unseen force in Casemate 5. This encounter also destroyed the inside of my 35 mm camera. Others have reported being hit in the stomach, pushed off the bunks, and we have also encountered objects thrown at us in this casemate. The identity of this spirit is not known.

We have also encountered and recorded the spirit of a man who identified himself as "Nate" here. Research revealed that a soldier named Nathan was beheaded in that area by a cannonball during the bombardment.

Casemate 11

This is a newly rediscovered area of the fort, which shows us the Fort Mifflin may still have secrets to reveal. It is believed to be the cell that held Union soldier and prisoner William Howe after he had led an attempted prison escape. He was held in this casemate, then sent to Eastern State, but was brought back to the fort for his execution. The spirits here are mistrustful of investigators and often refuse to communicate or ask to be left alone.

Other Areas

The sound of children laughing has been heard and recorded near the Artillery Shed. A woman in a blue dress that likes to shush people has been seen in the sally Port. The Torpedo Magazine is haunted by a young man, and the Soldier's Barracks are the location of phantom boot steps. The parade ground is frequented by a male spirit who likes to follow young women around.

Fort Mifflin is a place rich in history and paranormal activity. Many times when the visitors are few, I am struck by the thought that the unseen residents there far outnumber the flesh and blood people. If you are looking to have an experience, this place seldom disappoints. I say it is one spot where history really comes to life.

Entrance to Casemate 5.

Though it is difficult to see, there is a mist forming in front of the Soldier's Barracks. *Photo courtesy of Rich Hickman.*

Old Carbon County Jail - Jim Thorpe

I first visited the jail on a regular tour, not knowing that it was "haunted." I was interested in the historical aspect of the site, as this was where the Molly Maguires were hanged, and I wanted to see the reportedly indelible handprint on one of the walls. As I entered the main cell block area, I noticed that I was having difficulty breathing. I thought it was just my imagination, but the sensation persisted until I was outside of the jail. I was curious to see if I would experience this on a return visit. I had read an article entitled, "Restless Spirits," in the local paper about the jail that detailed experiences visitors had. Some visitors reported hearing voices, others reported being pushed or touched. No one had reported the sensation I experienced.

The Molly Maguires

This was a secret organization of Irish immigrants that was formed in the Coal Regions of Pennsylvania. The members of the organization were said to be responsible for several incidents of violence and intimidation that were directed towards the mining companies that employed and exploited them.

The Old Jail was similar in design to Eastern State Penitentiary in Philadelphia, and was designed by the son of the architect who designed Eastern State. It has one main cell block with a reconstructed gallows in the center. The solitary dungeon-like cells are in the basement. The main cellblock looks the same as it did when the Molly Maguires were held there in the late 1800s. The two rear cells were used for solitary confinement after 1979.

Prior to 1979, solitary cells were located in the basement. The basement is very damp, dark, and spooky. Lighting had to be installed before it was opened for tours, and the electrician who was hired to install the lights swore that he would never go back down there again. There are shackles still attached to some of the walls. Until laws were changed in 1979, prisoners were held in these dark, cold cells for up to two weeks at a time. It is so cold down there that tours do not go down there in winter. Each cell has a thick metal door with a small opening in the top. Only one of the eight basement cells has a toilet. Two of the Molly Maguires were said to have been held in these basement cells; James Kerrigan and Edward Kelly.

Cell 17

The main attraction, Cell 17, is on the main floor of the block. It is to the immediate left as one stands facing the reconstructed gallows. The wall of this cell bears the legendary handprint. Legend has it that the handprint was left by one of the accused Molly Maguires, either Alexander Campbell or Thomas Fisher. Before his execution, the convicted man put his hand on the dirt floor, then pressed it against the wall. He then stated that the mark would remain there forever as a sign of his innocence.

The handprint on the wall was first noticed after the execution. Since then, it has reportedly been washed, painted over, dug out, and plastered over, after which it is said to fade, but then returns. The handprint was also examined by a geologist and analyzed using a gas chromatograph. The only material that was detected was the paint on the wall.

Recently, this claim has been questioned. During an interview I conducted with Katharine Ramsland, local author and forensic investigator, she revealed that her research showed that the handprint itself was not subjected to any of these processes due to fear of permanently erasing it. The processes were carried out on the area right next to the handprint. Research of others has thrown into question whether the hand could even be attributed to the Molly Maguires. I will leave these arguments to the experts in this type of analysis, as whether the handprint was left by Alexander Campbell or some enterprising tour guide, has no bearing on whether the jail is haunted or not. In fact, none of the paranormal activity reported at the jail comes from Cell 17.

The Real Haunts

In conducting research into the jail history, I ran across many ghost stories and accounts of others who had experiences similar to mine at the jail. On one visit to the jail, I felt some unseen hand grab my left thigh as I walked down the steps into the women's section of the prison. As I concentrated and tried to pick up more information, I felt that a woman had been assaulted there and was still trying to get someone to listen to her and help her. I have talked to one other psychic who experienced the exact same touch and feeling in the same place.

Niehoff and More

I heard another ghost story associated with the jail; this came from someone on a genealogy website. This one dates from the late 1940s, and also centers on a man who claimed innocence, but was convicted anyway. A man was accused of murdering his brother, and was subsequently convicted and sentenced to life in prison. The man swore revenge on the Carbon County District attorney. He was sent to state prison to serve his sentence, and no one thought much of his threat until one night the man hung himself in his cell. His suicide note stated that he was going to haunt the Carbon County jail forever in protest of his unjust verdict. Supposedly, to prove his innocence, he would scratch the name "Niehoff" on the floor outside his old cell, Cell 2. The name appeared there, and is still there. Inmates and guards claimed that every year, on the anniversary of his suicide, the spirit could be heard scratching on the floor of the jail, in front of Cell 2. I do not know if this is true or not. The word "Niehoff" is on the floor in front of the cell, and Carl Niehoff was the district attorney there in the 1940s.

One other ghost at the jail lurks at the upper right corner of the second tier of cells. Many people who have entered this cell have reported feeling an uncomfortably tight restriction on their throat. Some of the tour guides have admitted that it is rumored that an inmate hung himself in that cell.

The jail seems to be full of history and spirits wanting their stories to be told. Every time we have visited the jail, someone in our group has had an experience. On our last visit, we had my young son with us and as we walked through the basement dungeon he leaned over in my arms, pointed at a cell and said, "There he is!" I looked over into a dark and completely empty cell. We continued with the tour and as we walked back past the cell, he said the same thing, "There he is!" and pointed at the empty cell.

I let him down to run around and he ran in a circle and came back, pointed at the cell again, calling out, "There he is!" One of the other people on the tour with us looked at me and said, 'That's pretty creepy." We didn't see anything, but it was obvious that my son did.

This location remains on my list of most haunted as well as my list of favorite historic places to visit.

The entrance to the Women's Block, where I felt a phantom touch.

The dungeon cell where
my son saw someone…
who wasn't there.

The suicide cell.

The jail was built in 1875 and is the oldest public building in Smethport. Currently it is a museum run by the McKean County Historical Society who shares the space with the ghost of a convicted murderer, Ralph Crossmire. According to legend he swore to return after his execution to haunt the prison where he spent his final hours on Earth. According to historical records, he was "asked ... if he had anything to say. [Crossmire] replied; "Father into Thy hands I commend my spirit." Then while the Sheriff held Ralph by the hand, the prisoner said: "I forgive all those who have sinned against me."[36]

If traumatic events can create permanent emotional imprints on an environment, then it makes sense that this jail is haunted. Ralph Crossmire was hanged in 1893 from a specially designed gallows that was built directly in front of his cell.

The crime he was convicted of committing was no less disturbing. He was convicted or murdering his own mother by beating her death with a heavy piece of wood and then hanging her body from a beam in the barn, where it was discovered by a seven-year-old boy.

In reading some of the records, it seems that the jail could be haunted by almost anyone. The unheated and unlit cells in what can only be referred to as a dungeon were used to house unruly prisoners. There was at least one suicide there, a man named Charles Rolander, who cut his own throat while he was imprisoned for assault with intent to kill. This grisly suicide could certainly be the beginning of a ghost story.

Crossmire was the third man hanged in McKean County Jail, but he was not the last. There were two others after him. All five were hanged after being convicted of murder. First was Uzza Robbins, who was convicted of poisoning his wife. "Uzza Robbins was hanged August 30, 1850, and buried, but during the night the earth was removed, the murderer's head cut off, and carried to a carpenter's shop, where it was found the next day, and replaced in the grave by a committee of citizens."[37] Then in 1905, the *Port Alleghany Reporter* newspaper published a story about a troubling discovery. "While John Grigsby was excavating in the rear of S. S. Fry's barn, near the corner of Water and Fulton Streets, last Tuesday, he uncovered a coffin, which upon being opened, was found to contain the skeleton of a man. From information obtained of old residents of the borough, there seems to be little doubt but that the remains are those of Uzza Robbins, the first person hanged in McKean County."[38] Disturbing a grave and decapitation are classic causes of a haunting. Could the ghost of the jail be Robbins?

The second was Andrew Tracy, a lawyer convicted of murdering his cousin, Mary Reilly. The testimony as reported in the newspapers was extensive. Apparently Mr. Tracy shot Mary dead in the street as she and her friend, Belle Mullin, ran from him in fear for their lives. Mary's father testified that Andrew had begun to be interested in Mary romantically. He had forbidden him to court Mary as they were cousins. Other witnesses testified that Andrew was insane and had been behaving strangely for some time prior to the murder; nevertheless he was executed on April 17, 1879. This murder and execution likely tore the entire family apart. Could what must have been an extremely high level of emotion surrounding this case cause Andrew Tracy to walk the jail in torment?

Of course, it is possible this jail is haunted by more than one spirit. The prisoner who occupied Crossmire's cell after his execution is said to have seen the ghost of the executed prisoner, so any ghostly appearances or activity at the jail are associated with him. Among the incidents attributed to Crossmire's ghost are a cellar light that turns on by itself, keys that appear in unusual places, and an overwhelming feeling of doom.

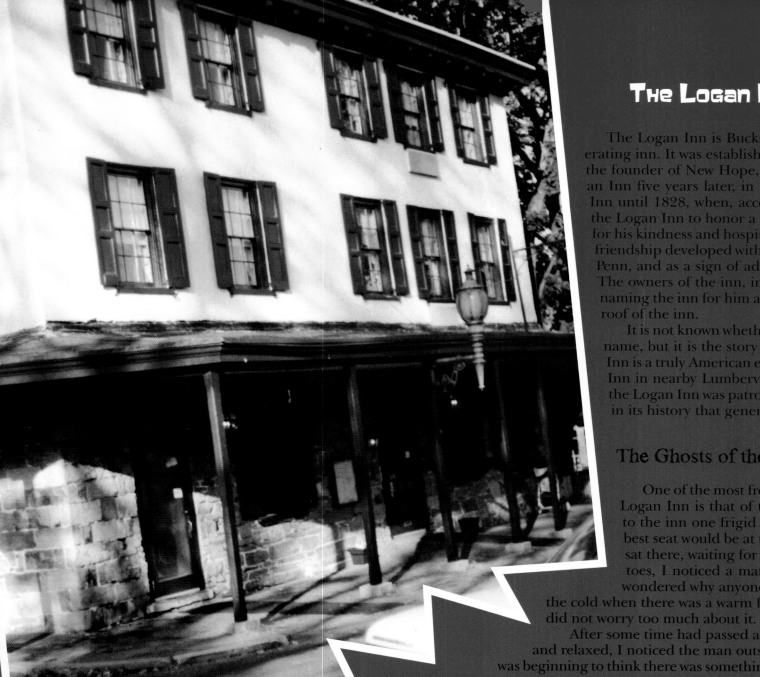

The Logan Inn - New Hope

The Logan Inn is Bucks County's oldest continuously operating inn. It was established in 1722 as The Ferry Tavern by the founder of New Hope, John Wells and entered service as an Inn five years later, in 1727. It was not called the Logan Inn until 1828, when, according to legend, it was re-named the Logan Inn to honor a local Lenape chief who was "noted for his kindness and hospitality with the white settlers. A close friendship developed with James Logan, secretary to William Penn, and as a sign of admiration Logan's name was taken. The owners of the inn, in turn, chose to honor the chief by naming the inn for him and placing a likeness of him on the roof of the inn.

It is not known whether this is the true origin of the inn's name, but it is the story the innkeepers prefer. The Logan Inn is a truly American establishment. While the Black Bass Inn in nearby Lumberville catered to the British soldiers, the Logan Inn was patronized by Patriots. It was this period in its history that generated two of its ghosts.

The Ghosts of the Tavern

One of the most frequently encountered ghosts at the Logan Inn is that of the colonial soldier. During a visit to the inn one frigid November evening, I decided the best seat would be at the table right next to the fire. As I sat there, waiting for my drink and trying to defrost my toes, I noticed a man standing by the door, outside. I wondered why anyone would choose to stand outside in the cold when there was a warm fire and lively company inside, but did not worry too much about it.

After some time had passed and I was feeling all warm and cozy and relaxed, I noticed the man outside the door again. At this point I was beginning to think there was something odd about it. It was dark outside, but suddenly he was very clear to me where he had been in shadow before. He was wearing a tricorn hat, a bulky jacket, and long trousers. Thinking it was possibly someone in a costume hat, I got up to see. I walked over to the door and opened it. The icy wind took my breath away as did the realization that there was no one out there.

Puzzled, I returned to my seat and went back to enjoying the atmosphere and conversation. I wasn't sure who he was or where he had gone. The tricorn hat was weird, but he had been wearing long trousers, not knee breeches, so maybe…

There he was again! He was standing just outside the door. I couldn't see him as clearly now, but the outline of his distinctive hat was clear. I kept watching and waiting for him to become clear again, but it didn't happen. He seemed to shift position every so often, but he never moved from the spot he was in. The impression I got was that he was waiting for someone or watching for something. The temptation to get up and try to get a closer look at him was overwhelming, but I had a feeling he would disappear if I approached. After a while we got up to leave and I looked to make sure he was still there. He was. I turned to say goodbye to the people we had chatted with and when I turned back he was gone.

I have not seen him on subsequent visits to the Logan, but when I asked a New Hope ghost tour guide about what I had seen, she nodded as I described him. He has been seen outside the door and in the bar, basement, and dining room of the Logan Inn. He is believed to have been a sentry, either waiting for someone he was meeting or acting as a look out for the Patriots inside. I asked her about his clothing, but she didn't remember anyone else commenting on the length of his trousers. Tradition at the inn holds that a wounded colonial soldier had been brought to the inn, where he died. Since it was winter and the ground was frozen, the body had to be stored in the basement until the thaw.

I described the man to a friend of mine who is a re-enactor. He said that my description would make the man a typical volunteer militia member. They had to furnish their own gear, so they would wear their everyday work or hunting clothing. He was especially interested in the bulky military-style jacket I saw, which he said sounded like it was a "Hudson Bay" jacket.

These were bulky coats that were actually made out of blankets.

The colonial soldier is not the only ghost in the basement area. Several times employees who have gone down to the basement to replenish supplies have almost run smack into a man wearing knee breeches. This man has also been reported on the stairs that lead to the men's room.

Employees have also reported hearing heavy, disembodied footfalls echo through the basement and full kegs of beer have mysteriously fallen over on their own. Most disconcerting is that from time to time an employee in the basement will suddenly find him or herself in total darkness when the lights unexpectedly turn off by themselves. Are these events the work of the soldier or is it the colonial man that stomps around, knocking over kegs and turning off the lights? Someday, I hope to get close enough to ask one of them.

The Ghosts of the Inn

The lobby of the Logan Inn is dominated by a large portrait of Charles and Elizabeth Lutz, the grandparents of a former owner of the inn.

One of the phenomena reported in the Inn is the smell of lavender. The source of the lavender was not known until one woman who admired the portrait pointed out that the woman in the portrait was wearing a sprig of lavender!

Charles and Elizabeth's daughter-in-law, Emily Lutz, is also said to haunt the inn. Her favorite room is Room 6. Emily makes her presence known by unlocking and opening the door in the middle of the night and pulling pillows out from under the heads of guests. One story told to me was that a businessman staying in Room 6 woke to pressure on his chest. When he opened his eyes, he saw a white, misty shape in the room. He promptly got up, dressed, and left in the middle of the night.

Women staying in "Emily's Room" have a different experience. Female guests in Room 6 have reported seeing the reflection of a man behind them in the bathroom mirror. When they turn around, there is no one there.

The haunted portrait. Note the lavender in her hair and on his coat.

The Sleepless Overnight

The Logan Inn is beautiful and historic and rumored to be haunted. I was so excited when I finally had the opportunity to stay overnight there. Room 6 was not available, but I was assured by the person on the phone that "the entire inn is haunted." We were given Room 7, the room directly across from Room 6.

I had been to New Hope so many times that I knew all the ghost stories of Ferry Street by heart. I walked my husband up one side of Ferry Street and down the other, telling him the tales of sorrowful spirits and unfinished business. He patiently listened and as we walked back towards the inn, I knew he was glad to reach the room. At that time he was not a believer in ghosts. The spirits at the Logan Inn were about to change all that. I was thrilled to be finally spending the night there and had originally had a grand plan of holding a vigil, I fell asleep.

I woke in the darkness, shaking with cold. I was shocked that I couldn't see my breath. Then I realized that I was looking into the face of a sleeping man who was not my husband. I was lying on my side, facing the wall. Right next to me, facing me, was a man with reddish brown hair and a spade-shaped beard. He was lying on his left side, sleeping. He was lying as if on a bed, slightly higher than the bed I was on. He was floating in the air, over the space between my bed and the wall. For a few seconds I thought I was dreaming. When I realized I was actually experiencing the presence of something supernatural, I slowly slid down to the bottom of the bed, trying not to disrupt the scene. I was headed for my camera. As I reached the chair where my bag was placed, my husband suddenly sat up in bed.

"What's going on?" he asked. "It's freezing in here…" His voice trailed off as he glanced around the room and saw me with my camera in hand. I looked towards where I had been sleeping. The man was gone.

"Is there something going on here?" my husband inquired. "Seriously, Laurie, it feels like a freezer in here. Is something in here?"

As I related to him what I had seen, the room slowly returned to normal temperature. For some reason, this experience convinced my husband that ghosts exist and he is positive that one was with us in that room. I stayed awake the rest of the night, willing the man to return, but the moment had passed. I was too pumped with adrenaline from the whole experience to sleep and I know my husband was awake, too nervous from his first real brush with the paranormal.

I have not stayed in the Inn again, but have passed it many times as I walked up or down Ferry Street. As I pass by, I can never resist the urge to glance up at the window of Room 7 and wonder who the mysterious auburn-haired gentleman was that shared his room with us that night.

I recently received a report of another experience at the Logan Inn. This was related to me by Brooke Andrew Miller who was visiting from Texas and had the good fortune of staying in Room 6. When she first entered the room after checking in, she was pleased with it and noticed nothing unusual. She went downstairs to the bar for a bit and when she returned to the room to change for dinner, the entire room smelled very strongly of lavender perfume. She just knew that someone had been in her room. The thought of ghosts crossed her mind, but there didn't seem to be anyone there now, so she went and took a shower. When she was done, she stood at the sink to brush her teeth and saw an older man staring at her in the mirror. Of course she quickly turned around only to see an empty room. She went to her friend's room to tell them what she saw and he came back to the room with her to look around. Seeing nothing amiss, they left for dinner after locking the door.

When she returned to the room, the ladies in their party went upstairs to bed so it was just Brooke and two of the men who returned to her room to play cards. While they were in the room, the doors to the armoire began to shake. One of the guys got up, opened the doors and yelled for whoever it was to stop. That worked because the doors stopped shaking.

When the card game was finished they all decided to turn in for the night. She was alone in the room getting ready for bed and the room got extremely cold. Again, she asked whoever it was to leave her alone and again it seemed to work, but being a little nervous, she left the television on and put the remote on the bed table. The next morning, the TV was off and the remote control was in the bathroom sink.

As they headed out to their car in the parking lot behind the inn they noticed a beer bottle sitting on the step of the parking attendant booth. One of the guys remarked that someone must have had a party out here last night. Brooke acknowledged his statement and when she turned around to look back at the inn the beer bottle suddenly flew across the parking lot like someone picked it up and threw it. Funny thing was, there was not a soul in sight.

This is why the Logan Inn is considered one of the most haunted places in Pennsylvania. There are continuous and consistent reports of paranormal activity and experiences there. Next time you are in the area, book a room there. Then you may be able to add your own experience to the lore of the Logan Inn.

Logan Inn
10 West Ferry Street
New Hope, PA
www.loganinn.com

Hawk Mountain Sanctuary - Ecksville/Kempton

This area on the Kittatinny Ridge of the Appalachian Mountains is a well known site for hiking, bird watching, and experiencing the paranormal. The first people to recognize the special energy of this area were the Lenape, who constructed what appears to be a medicine wheel on the mountain.

A medicine wheel is constructed by the laying out of rocks or stones in a pattern that looks like a cross section of a wheel. The location for these structures is believed to have been chosen due to the location's particular energy. Some people theorize that these sacred sites are located on ley lines, which are pathways that connect sacred sites. The lines or pathways can be revealed or found by dowsing. These circles are believed to have ceremonial or astronomical significance.

When the English and German settlers arrived in the area and began to establish communities, their efforts were sometimes met with resistance by the Native population as well as the French fur traders, who had already established a thriving trade throughout the Northeast United States. The French and English had an uneasy alliance when they had one and their bitterness towards each other continued in the colonies and eventually erupted into the French and Indian War. Tensions ran high in the period leading up to the war and there were several raids on English settlements and Native villages.

One of these raids occurred on Hawk Mountain on February 7, 1756, when the Gerhardt family was attacked in their cabin, which was located at the foot of Hawk Mountain at Ecksville. The entire family was murdered; the father, the mother, and six children, and the house was burned.[39] The only survivor was 12-year-old Jacob Gerhardt, who escaped from the burning building by jumping from a window. "Jacob Gerhardt, Jr., moved into an existing building that is now Schaumbach's Tavern, near what is now the Hawk Mountain Sanctuary".[40] The area is said to be haunted by the Gerhardt family, victims of that long ago raid.

After Jacob, the building was owned by Matthias Schaumbach, who is referred to in a few sources as a murderous innkeeper, who would get his guests intoxicated and the murder them. He would them steal their

A medicine wheel at a psychic development center

belongings and bury their remains on the property. This was not discovered until Matthias made a death-bed confession in which he claimed he was compelled to commit these murders by some evil energy that lurked in the forest.

Hikers and visitors to the area have reported seeing balls of light, hearing disembodied wails and being suddenly overcome by a feeling of unease. I have received several reports of unusual occurrences experienced by visitors, and have received some interesting photos. The most commonly reported photographic anomaly here is that photos seem to capture some type of swirling vortex effect that causes a blur in a circular pattern.

One very interesting photo was sent to me that captured what appears to be a human-shaped, blurry, rainbow.

The most commonly reported phenomena here is that of unexplained noises and sounds.

One man reported that he and his brother were walking his dog along the state game land trail when they heard a loud "whoomp" off in the trees above them on the mountain. The only thing he could think of that makes a similar sound is something heavy hitting the ground. It spooked them, so they decided to return to their car. They heard it again as they were walking, and after a bit they stopped to listen, and heard it again, only now it was ahead of them but still coming from above. It seemed like it was following them, but they didn't hear any sounds of something moving through the trees. They were experienced hunters and were very familiar with the sounds that deer, people, or squirrels make when moving through brush. This wasn't any of those things. Most disturbing of all was that the dog, which usually enjoyed walks in the wild, seemed equally keen to get out of there. When they got back to their vehicle, they were the only car in the lot. They have no idea what they heard that day, but they know it was not something normally heard on that mountain.

If you go to Hawk Mountain, make sure you have a camera and a recorder ready. You never know how the spirits of the mountain will make themselves known.

A rainbow man joins this hiker as he walks the trails of Hawk Mountain. *Photo courtesy of Lori Clark.*

The beautiful view from Hawk Mountain.
Photo courtesy of Lori Clark.

HISTORIC HOME IN CONCORD, PENNSYLVANIA

Of all the historic homes I have had the privilege of investigating, this home has the most activity and is the most interesting. We and the residents have experienced the full range of paranormal phenomena, including disembodied footsteps, phantom touches, unexplained voices, poltergeist activity, olfactory phenomena, and full-body apparitions. The family that lives here truly enjoys the history and unseen residents of their home and has always tried to understand them and treat them as part of the family.

When we first drove up to the house, we saw someone watching from the third-floor window. As we were introduced to some of the family members, we asked if there was anyone upstairs. They said, "No." We had already seen the first of many spirits that inhabited the old farm.

That preliminary investigation and the others that followed revealed at least six different intelligent spirits in the house. The two that have appeared as full-body apparitions are a tall, thin, a man dressed in black and a young girl who appears to be about twelve years old. The man stayed mainly on the second floor, near the office and on the left side of the house. The man of the house said that many, many times when he was working in that office the door would open on its own. He would get upset because he didn't want to air condition the whole hallway, so he told the spirit man to stop, and he had no more problems after that.

I saw the man in the hallway outside the office and also smelled a strong odor of pipe smoke in the bathroom next to the office. No one in the house smokes and they reported that many of them have also smelled that same odor in that area.

The spirit of the twelve-year-old girl appeared to two of the daughters while they were sleeping in their parents' bedroom. She appeared at the foot of the bed, staring at them in a way that they did not feel was friendly. One night, in the same area where the girl had appeared, the mother observed the brass handle on the dresser move up and then drop down by itself. We have recorded unusual temperature fluctuations and EMF fluctuations in that same area.

Things were most interesting on the third floor when we walked towards the window we had observed someone watching us from. As I stepped near the window, we were pushed back by a rush of energy that let out an audible whooshing or sighing sound that sounded like something out of

The sound of a baby crying was heard here.

One of these lids popped off and flew across the
table in this colonial-era kitchen.

a Halloween haunted house. While we tried to figure out where it came from or what it was, I heard a baby crying. When we reviewed the audio from that night the sighing sound was actually saying, "Get out of my house." Incredibly, the sound of the baby crying appeared on the audio as well, followed by the voice of a woman whispering, "No, no, no," as if she were trying to get the baby to stop crying.

The family seemed not to be surprised by everything we had experienced. I suppose to them it was another day at their house. They did tell us that one of the daughters in the house had a baby out of wedlock and it had been a huge scandal at the time. She became such an outcast in the family that she was not even buried in the same section of the cemetery as the rest of her relatives. Subsequent communications revealed that she was so very sorry for breaking her father's heart. I felt such sympathy for this poor girl. We told her that we knew about the baby and so did the family that lives there and they did not think badly of her; in fact they loved her and enjoyed her company.

The other spirits there were a man in the basement named Joseph, a man by the side of the property, and a nanny who still checks on people that sleep on the third floor. The family told us that there was a Joseph that lived there and spent his life working on the farm. They feel that this might be the Joseph in the basement.

While we sat discussing various experiences the family had in the house, I related a similar experience that I had at my house. I then told the story of the non-believing friend who was treated to a flying cookie tin. As soon as I finished the story, a lid from a jar behind me popped off, flew up in the air next to me, and landed across the table. I was amazed that not only had the spirits been listening to us, but they were interacting with us and wanted to make their point. The family barely reacted at all to the flying lid. Their comment was, "Things like that happen all the time."

A few things have happened over the years that frightened children in the house, but as they grew up, they seemed to be more interested, like we were, in trying to understand the purpose behind the events they witnessed. One very dramatic event occurred one night when the children were home alone. One of the older girls got up with the youngest baby to get him a bottle and while she was making it, she heard a loud pounding at the kitchen door. There was a fierce storm outside, so, thinking it was a stranded motorist she looked out the window. There was no one there.

Suddenly a loud pounding started on the front door. Terrified, she ran to get her siblings. They all witnessed the phantom knocker pass from one door to the next, pounding on each of the six doors on the first floor. They never saw anyone out there, so they called a relative who lived nearby. The relative arrived, checked the house and even called the police to come and make sure everything was okay. There was no sign of anyone anywhere around.

The oddest thing about that night did not occur to them until they got older. If it was a stranger looking for help, how would they know where all the doors were all the way around? Wouldn't most people have stopped after the front and back door? They feel it was someone that knew where the doors were, someone that used to live there long ago. Perhaps it was a re-enactment of some past event, the recording or residual energy set off by the storm.

Most of us can only imagine what it must be like to live in a home that is haunted by so many different spirits that link the present residents with the past history of the house they live in. The family living there is so kind and hospitable, I don't blame the ghosts one bit for not wanting to leave.

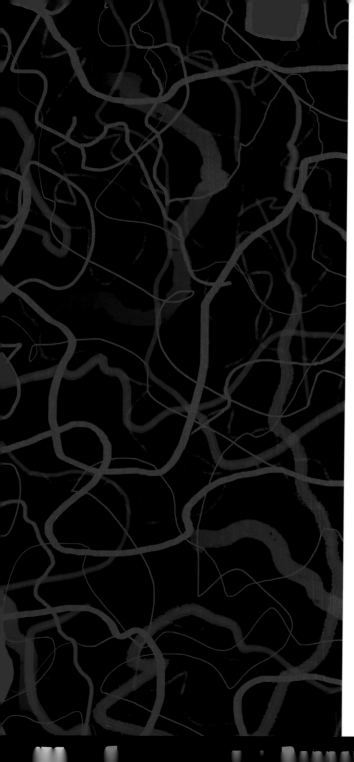

Conclusion

WARNING:

This Book May Be Haunted!

Having spent most of my life living in a haunted house, I am used to strange and un-explained things happening. Investigating and writing about the paranormal seems to add an extra layer of unexplained events to my life. More strange things have happened during the writing process of these books than have happened during an overnight at Fort Mifflin! Supernatural Pennsylvania has now set a new benchmark for weirdness. Files refused to save and then mysteriously changed names. Photos disappeared and had to be retaken, only to disappear again. Strange shadows flitted by as I was writing. I got a new computer and things got worse! Large parts of the manuscript would be written or edited by some unseen hand. This was especially true during the section about Spooky Cemeteries. I was never so glad to turn a manuscript in to my editor, Dinah. I thought to myself, "Whew! At least that strangeness was finished." My relief was short-lived. Shortly after Dinah began editing the book, she began experiencing similar issues.

Dinah Roseberry says:

As I was working on Laurie's book, things became "strange." It's not that things weren't strange enough in my office since most of my time is spent with ghost stories and other para-normal issues that Schiffer authors drop at my doorstep. But the first week I worked on Laurie's book was mind boggling. The initial glimpse into madness came after I'd begun editing her book and was a good six hours into her stories and setup – in other words, I'd spend a great deal of my time working on the book. Learning the hard way before (as most of us had), I saved my work frequently so that an unexpected power failure or other nasty malady would not steal all the work I'd done. Everything was saved to both a network and to my hard drive.

I'd like to say that it was a dark and stormy "day," but it wasn't. It was sun shiny and warm. Not a cloud in the sky and the atmosphere was bright and cheery. Except in my office. That should've been my first clue. But hindsight and all those clichés... Suddenly, as I looked at the screen, her manuscript was *POOF* gone. I narrowed my eyes. That did not just happen. I grumbled as I went to my local drive to open up the file again. It was not there. Frowning, I went to the network drive. It was not there. No. It had to be there. I was just working on it. My subconscious was whispering to me, "Don't panic. It has to be there." Then it began to shout, "That was six hours of work! And it's gone!" So I went to the original materials file. At least I would have Laurie's original work. I would just have to start over. This wasn't the end of the world. Worse things had happened. I'd had ghosts do things in my office before. I was sure it would not be the last time. I was not prepared for her original materials to be gone as well. The whole file was gone. How was that possible?

I called our IT guy, Ian. He was a master and could work wonders. I knew that he backed up files every night and was sure I'd at least have access to my work from the night before. But though he looked and looked—nothing related to Supernatural Pennsylvania was on the network. That was just nuts. Okay. I gathered myself. Worst-case scenario, Laurie would have a copy of her manuscript.

So I called Laurie to ask her to send me her copy. Was I surprised to hear that her copy had disappeared, too? Okay, now it was time to panic.

It was then that Ian found a copy of the manuscript—three megs of text saved as a photograph ... I didn't even know that was possible. So he changed it back to text—all my formatting was gone and had to be re-done, but at least it was there.

The next day, all copies in all places were back ...some sense of humor—but we think it was the work of the one whose name cannot be said...

Back to Laurie:

I did have a copy of the manuscript when she'd called, but strangely, it was not the manuscript I turned in. It was an earlier, longer manuscript that had needed cutting down. I went to get the backup copies that I e-mail to myself, save on a flash drive, and also on CD.

The e-mail copy was gone. It wasn't even in the deleted items folder! In fact, none of the copies that I e-mail myself daily were anywhere in my inbox, outbox, or recycle bin. Okay, well this was why I have it on CD as well. The CD was blank. This was getting really, really weird. I ejected the CD and tried it on another computer. It was there, but would not open, the file was corrupted. In the meantime, Dinah had contacted me and let me know that she found the manuscript saved as a photo. We hope that the strange events that accompanied the writing and editing of this book are limited to that process, but we cannot know for sure until others begin reading it.

+++++++++

Developing Psychic Abilities

One of the questions I am asked the most is:
"How can I develop my psychic abilities?"

The answer is simple but requires a commitment of time and energy on the part of the seeker. The first thing you must do is confront your own fears. Explore them, determine their source, and release them. In order to move forward in psychic development, one must be free from fear. Fear is a sign that the seeker is not yet ready to move forward and must attend to a blockage of some kind. Fear is a natural response that our bodies and minds give us in order to protect us. For example, humans rely mainly on sight to function, so when an area is dark; it is natural to be apprehensive at the deprivation of our primary ability.

The other thing that one must do is meditate. Meditation must be a daily habit in order to develop psychic abilities. Meditation helps you to know yourself, purify yourself, and be more aware of the spirit world. Meditate on dedication and commitment. Is this something you are afraid of? Is this something you welcome? Why? Allow your mind to explore your feelings, images, or whatever comes to you.

It is not uncommon to encounter images or feelings that are upsetting or frightening to you during meditation, especially if you are just beginning. This is a kind of test. If one flees from the fear, then fear wins. If we work through the fear and show that our desire for understanding is greater than our fear, then the doors to understanding will open for us.

You are already in communication with your guides and other ancestral spirits! Guides give us nudges to go to certain places, talk to certain people, or even warnings or ideas for solving problems. These things will initially come to us in dreams and as we get better at meditation, they will come through during meditation. Messages from your spirit guides will always be comforting, uplifting, empowering, loving, and positive. You should come away from meditation feeling enlightened, unburdened, and relaxed.

To boost your faith and courage and establish positive expectations, read uplifting books and spend time with other spiritual people. Other ways of raising your vibration include making a list of your blessings; people that you love unconditionally, or compliments you have received. As you meditate, visualize a bright white light coming from within yourself and surrounding your body. Extend it out so that it fills the room. Pick an affirmation that works for you, such as "I am a radiant being, filled with light and love." When you are ready, reach out with your mind and ask for your guide to approach you. Try to see the guide and feel his or her presence. Draw what you see or write down a description. This should be the start of an ongoing journal that you should keep to track your progress.

Understand that each of us is a unique individual with different gifts. No gift is better or worse than another. You have received the psychic gift that is right for you. Some people can see spirits, others can hear them, some can do both. Some people can tune into the emotions of people, animals, or spirits. Others are healers. Your meditations and communications with your guide will help you find your gift and develop it to its fullest potential.

Paranormal Groups

Tri County Paranormal
Serving Pennsylvania, New Jersey, and Delaware
www.tricountyprs.com

South Jersey Ghost Research
Serving New Jersey, Eastern Pennsylvania, Delaware, and New York City
www.sjgr.org

Allegheny Mountain Ghosthunters
Western Pennsylvania
www.amghosthunters.com

Atlantic Coast Paranormal Research Society
Philadelphia
/atlanticcoastprs.com/

Spirited Ghost Hunting
Ellwood City
www.spiritedghosthunting.com/

Eastern Pennsylvania Paranormal Society
Bath
eppsinvestigations.com/

The Pennsylvania Paranormal Association
www.theppa.net/

NEPA Paranormal
Wilkes-Barre
www.nepaparanormal.com/

Spirit Society of PA
Camp Hill
www.spiritsocietyofpa.com/

Ghost Hunters of Southern Tioga
Mansfield
www.ghostpa.com/

Central Pennsylvania Paranormal Research Association (CPPRA)
Danville
www.thecppra.com/

City Lights Paranormal Society
Easton
clps.weebly.com/

Central Pennsylvania Paranormal Research Association
Coal Region Chapter – Shamokin
www.coalregionghosts.com/

Complete Paranormal Services – Codorus
www.cpsparanormal.com/

G & K Paranormal Investigations
www.gkparanormalinvestigation.com/

Ghost Hunters Incorporated – Sinking Spring
www.ghosthuntersinc.net/

Paranormal Investigators of Chambersburg
Chambersburg
www.pitchparanormal.com/

Paranormal/Unexplained Researched Events Team
Petersburg
www.paranormaleventteam.com/default.html

Quest Paranormal Society
Reading
www.questparanormalsociety.com

Reading Paranormal Society
Reading
readingparanormalsociety.com/

Rogue Paranormal
Sharpsville
www.rogueparanormal.com/

Southeast Paranormal Investigation and Research Team
Philadelphia
www.spirtofpa.com/

Sparks Spirit Hunters
Hermitage
sparksspirithunters.com/

Steel Town Paranormal
Pittsburgh
www.steeltownparanormal.com/index.php?p=1_1

Midnight Watchmen
Perkasie
www.midnightwatchmen.com/

End Notes

Works Cited:

1. Roman Catholic Diocese of Pittsburgh website archives. http://www.diopitt.org/archives/January_1.htm.
2. Dudiak, Zandy. "If one believes – Area is rich with settings for the supernatural". *Penn Trafford Star*. October 24, 2007.
3. Ordine, Bill. *Knight Rider Newspapers*. *The New Orleans Times-Picayune*. August 22, 1999.
4. *Doylestown Daily Intelligencer*. December 15, 1932. Page 8.
5. The *New York Times*. May 31, 1935. Accessed at: http://www.ancestry.com.
6. Wardell, Lindy Constance, ed. Darby Images of America: Darby Borough. Borough Historical and Preservation Society. Arcadia Publishing, December 8, 2003.
7. The Electric Law Library at: http://www.lectlaw.com/def2/p139.htm.
8. Lancaster County Department of Parks and Recreation website. http://www.co.lancaster.pa.us/parks/cwp/view.asp?a=676&q=518276.
9. Associated Press. *St. Petersburg Times*. "Murder Swamp Yields Another Mutilated Body." November 3, 1940.
10. Ibid.
11. The Stottsville Inn Website: http://www.stottsville.com/.
12. *Coatesville-West Chester Times*. July 8, 1893.
13. Chester County Death Records. http://publicrecords.onlinesearches.com/PA_Chester.htm.
14. Meigs, Henry B. "Record of the Descendents of Vincent Meigs," 1901, page 234.
15. Directory of Deceased American Physicians, 1804 – 1929.
16. http://www.archives.upenn.edu/people/1700s/chew_ben.html.
17. http://www.nemacolincastle.org/history.html.
18. http://freepages.history.rootsweb.ancestry.com/~glenntunneycolumn/capsule302.htm.
19. http://www.brittinghams.com/history.php.
20. Ibid.
21. Lehighton Chamber of Commerce. The Lehighton Story. 1955.
22. Henry, M.S. History of the Lehigh Valley. 1864.
23. *New York Times* (1857 – Current file); July 26, 1895; ProQuest Historical Newspapers. *New York Times* (1857 – 2005) Page 1.
24. Ibid.
25. *New York Times* (1857 – Current file); April 6, 1896. ProQuest Historical Newspapers. *New York Times* (1857 – 2005). Page 2.
26. Ibid.
27. *New York Times* (1857 – Current file); November 3, 1895. ProQuest Historical Newspapers. *New York Times* (1857 – 2005). Page 3.
28. *New York Times* (1857 – Current file); July 26, 1895. ProQuest Historical Newspapers. *New York Times* (1857 – 2005). Page 2.
29. Ibid.
30. *New York Times* (1857 – Current file); April 6, 1896. ProQuest Historical Newspapers. *New York Times* (1857 – 2005). Page 2.
31. Ibid.
32. William Morrison. The Main Line Country Houses. Acanthus Press. 2004. Page 149.
33. Zimmerman, Chelsea. "Bizarre Things about Eastern: Eastern Ghosts." *The Waltonian*. October 2006.
34. Council of Independent Colleges: Historic Campus Architecture Project website. http://puka.cs.waikato.ac.nz/cgi-bin/cic/library?a=d&d=p1987.
35. Haining, Peter. *A Dictionary of Ghost Lore*. Prentice Hall. 1984.
36. Historic McKean County Jail website. http://www.smethporthistory.org/king.street/jail/jail.index.htm.
37. "History of the Counties of McKean, Elk, Cameron and Potter, PA with Biographical Selections"; J. H. Beers and Co., 1890.
38. *The Port Alleghany Reporter*, October 20, 1905. "A Gruesome Find at Smethport – Said to be Bones of Uzza Robbins."
39. Montgomery, Morton. *History of Berks County in Pennsylvania. Philadelphia*. Everts, Peck & Richards, 1886.
40. Rupp, Daniel. *History of Lehigh County*. G. T. Hawbaker. 1845.

The Pennsylvania Paranormal Association
Scranton
www.theppa.net/

The Supernatural Research Group
Reading
www.tsrg.org/

Tri State Area Paranormal Research and Investigation
Philadelphia
www.tapri.org/

True Hauntings Pennsylvania Paranormal Investigations
Bloomsburg
truehauntingspaparanormal.club.officelive.com/default.aspx

West Pennsylvania Paranormal Investigations Group
Ellwood City
west-pa-ghosts.blogspot.com/

York County Paranormal Research Team
York
www.ycprt.com/

Bibliography

Ashmead, Henry Graham, and William Shaler Johnson. *Historical Sketch of Chester on Delaware*. Republican Steam Printing. Chester, 1883.

Ashmead, Henry Graham. *History of Delaware County, Pennsylvania*. L. H. Everts & Co. Philadelphia, 1884.

Associated Press. "Chester Footbridge Collapses into River," The *New York Times*, New York September 11, 1921.

Butterfield, Roger P. (5 March 1933). "The Hangman Who Didn't Wait." *Philadelphia: Public Ledger*.

Chester Times. "3rd Street Bridge Collapse Claimed 24 Lives in 1921." *Chester Times*, September 1951.

Chester Times, The. "Slain Man's Garments May Lead to Identity". April 5, 1930.

Chester Times, The. "Headless Murder, in Pittsburgh, Solved". April 10, 1930.

Columbo, John Robert. *Windigo: An Anthology Of Fact And Fantastic Fiction*. Saskatoon, Western Producer Prairie Books, 1982.

Delaware County Courthouse Public Access at http://w01.co.delaware.pa.us/pa/publicaccess.asp.

History of American Women at http://womenhistory.blogspot.com/2009/01/elizabeth-graeme-fergusson.html.

Lansdowne Borough. www.lansdowneborough.com.

Larsen, Erik. *The Devil in the White City*. Vintage Books. 2004.

McKean County Miner, The. The Great Trial – Commonwealth Vs. Andrew Tracy. February 27, 1879.

Morriseau, Norval. *Legends Of My People: The Great Odjibway*. McGraw-Hill Ryerson, 1977.

New Hope Ghost Tours at http://www.ghosttoursofnewhope.com/

O'Hanlon-Lincoln, Ceane. *County Chronicles: A Vivid Collection of Fayette County, Pennsylvania Histories*. Mechling Bookbindery, 2004.

Reichel, William C., ed. *Memorials of the Moravian Church. Vol. 1*. J.B. Lippincott & Co. Philadelphia, 1870.

Sagar, Kate Day. "Jail has eternal inmate." *Olean Times Herald*. October 29, 2008.

Treese, Lorett. *Graeme Park*. Stackpole Books, 2003.

Wedgwood Inn at http://www.wedgwoodinn.com/.

Index